To Mike

I hope you enjoy
my book!

THE ANXIOUS
LANGUAGE
LEARNER

A Saudi Woman's Story

TAGHREED M. AL-SARAJ, Ph.D.

© Taghreed M. Al Saraj, 2017
King Fahad National Library Cataloging-in-Publication Data

Al Saraj, Taghreed M.
   The anxious language learner: a Saudi womans story./
   Taghreed M. Al Saraj .- Jeddah, 2017

   198 Pages: 16 x 24 cm
ISBN: 978-603-02-5805-5

1- Language and languages - Study and teaching - Physchological aspects
2- Second language acquisition   I-Title

   401.93 dc   1439/1912

   L.D. no. 1439/1912
   ISBN: 978-603-02-5805-5

ISBN: 978-0-9861327-3-5

Library of Congress Control Number: 2015903030

Printed in Kingdom of Saudi Arabia

Published by Educate Right, Ltd.

www.EducateRight.com

www.ForeignLanguageAnxiety.net (Blog and FLA Discussion Site)

First Printing 2015

Cover by TotenCreative

THE ANXIOUS LANGUAGE LEARNER

A Saudi Woman's Story

TAGHREED M. AL-SARAJ, Ph.D.

To my beloved husband Fouad for his support, encouragement, and patience in helping me follow my inquiring mind and satisfy my curiosity for knowledge and research.

The unconditional love I have received from my three wonderful boys, Rayan, Kenan, and Aban, has kept me going so that I could set a good example for them. The journey of obtaining knowledge never ends, even for a mother who, in her children's eyes, knows everything!

I praise my father, Mohammed, who instilled in my three siblings and me the value of education. I praise my mother, Huda (a high school principal), who modeled valuing education for us by continuing her education even after she married at a very young age.

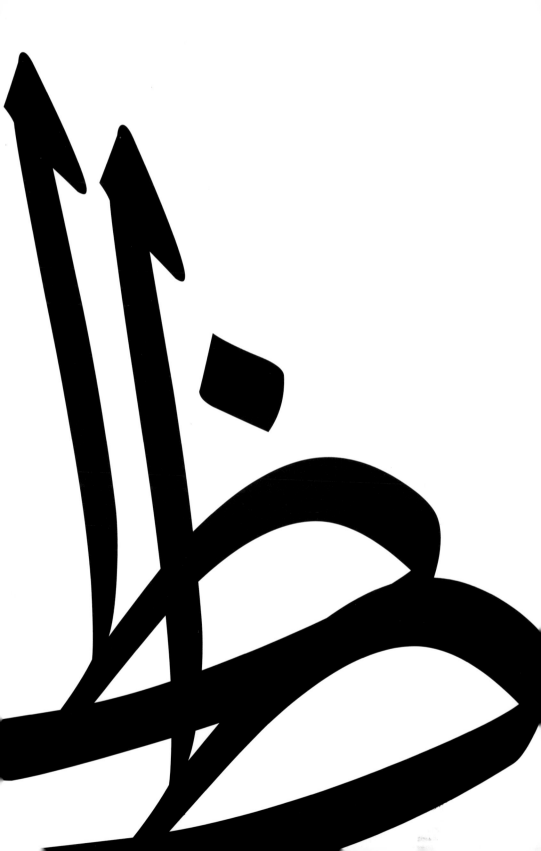

Table of Contents

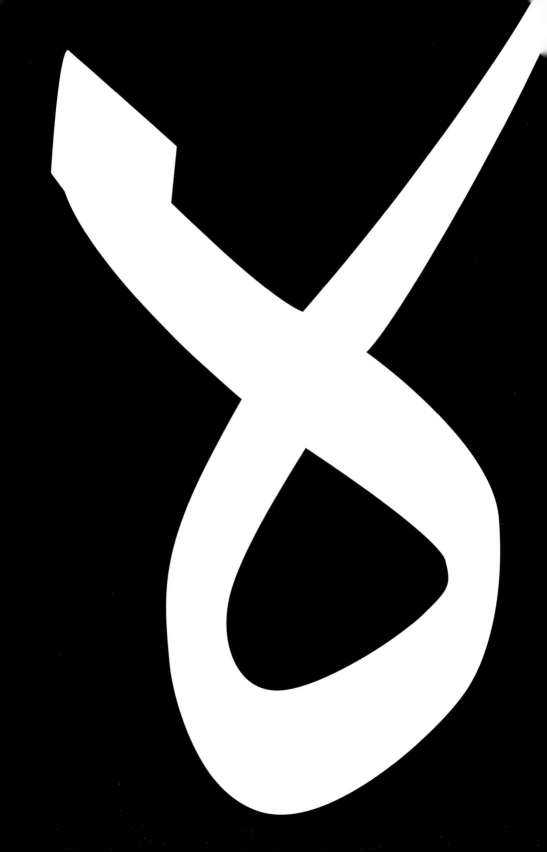

Praise for The Anxious Language Learner

"This book will ignite your passion to learn something new—if not a new language then something else—because the author's passion for learning is contagious. The author's writing style makes the book appealing to different types of readers. *The Anxious Language Learner* combines storytelling with practical tips for both teachers and students in the language education field. Dr. Taghreed is an example and proof of the increasing number of talented Saudi women who are succeeding in many fields in the 21st century."

—Ahmad Alshugairi
Host of Khawater, a popular Arabic TV Program

"A splendid book! If you're learning a second language, The Anxious Language Learner will empower and encourage you. Before reading this book, I never thought about foreign language anxiety. Now, I realize I have it, but am inspired by the author's personal example to continue on, and to use her techniques to overcome my anxiety. If you're learning a second language, I highly recommend this book."

—*Ghadeer Attallah*
Foreign Language Student, Architect & Urban planner

"I tremendously enjoyed reading The Anxious Language Learner: A Saudi Woman's Story. It is an easy-flowing book and unquestionably a page-turner. Dr. Al Saraj provides both an account of her personal struggle in learning a foreign language, as well as a proficient piece of scientific evidence about foreign language anxiety. This is an invitation for language teachers to delve into themselves and see what hurdles they might have experienced while learning a foreign language—in order to identify with what their students might be going through."

—*Mariam Chanbour Ghalayini*
Director, University Academic Preparation Program
Dar Al Hekma University

"Nearly every paragraph in this book is inspirational. Not only is language anxiety an interesting topic, but the spirit of the author and her love of knowledge is inspiring. Dr. Al-Saraj addresses one of the most common problems in the lives of language learners, and provides creative solutions as a recipe to alleviate the suffering that affects those learning a foreign language."

—Motlag Alanzi
Managing Editor, Alyaum Newspaper
Saudi Arabia

"Dr. Taghreed's approach to the topic of foreign language anxiety is outstanding: She addresses the issue of foreign language anxiety through physical and emotional symptoms as well as culturally-sensitive surveys. And, she challenged herself to experience the language-learning process so she could understand foreign language anxiety firsthand. Her enthusiasm and dedication are deeply felt throughout the book."

—Emin Bostancioglu
English Instructor
Yildiz Technical University, Istanbul, Turkey

About the Author

As an English language lecturer at Dar Al-Hekma College in Jeddah, Saudi Arabia, Taghreed M. Al-Saraj, Ph.D., saw firsthand the debilitating effects of Foreign Language Anxiety (FLA) on Saudi Arabian language students. Her observations drove her to research the reasons that Saudi language students experience anxiety while learning a new language. In addition, she now recognizes her own anxiety-related language learning experiences, and works to raise teachers' awareness of FLA, as well as educate them about strategies to lessen the impact of this anxiety on their students.

Dr. Al-Saraj is now serving as the first female Saudi Arabian Post Doctorate fellow at University of California, Berkeley. She earned both her bachelor's and master's degrees in Teaching English as a Foreign Language (TEFL) from the University of Miami, graduating with highest honors, and went on to earn her Ph.D. in 2011 from University College of London, Institute of Education.

To spread the word about FLA, Dr. Al-Saraj lectures on this topic in the Middle East and at international conferences around the world. She's considered a leading Saudi researcher in the field of FLA in the Middle East, and has published her research in top international journals, including *Innovations in Language Learning*, the *International Journal of Bilingual Education and Bilingualism*, and the *L2 Journal*, in addition to being a reviewer for leading journals in the field.

In addition to her passion for the study of FLA, Dr. Al-Saraj is also driven to raise money for cancer research, so much so that she once ran in "Race for Life," the largest women-only fundraising event in the UK, while fasting during the Muslim holy month of Ramadan. She also served as the only female Saudi Arabian London Ambassador for the 2012 London Olympics, Her Western friends call her an unofficial Saudi ambassador, and she loves speaking about and representing her beloved country in the West. A "self-driven Saudi woman," Dr. Al-Saraj currently lives in the San Francisco area.

Foreword

I met Dr. Taghreed Al-Saraj when I served as the internal examiner at the viva of her Ph.D., the oral exam at which a doctoral candidate is grilled about her dissertation. Since Taghreed had acquired English, her second language, as a child, I later joked that she had never really experienced the foreign language anxiety she had studied so intently.

Taghreed loves challenges, so I wasn't surprised when she told me she had developed a passion for Turkish and had decided to study it formally. She's become not only a researcher of foreign language anxiety, but also a subject of her own study.

I enjoyed reading Taghreed's thesis, and was struck by its originality. Her work explored foreign language anxiety using a questionnaire specifically designed for the Saudi Arabian context, allowing her to gain unique insights into the nature of this anxiety in her home country. In addition, it combined hard, quantitative data and observations of individuals' experiences—crucial in discovering patterns and understanding the human experience of foreign language anxiety.

Since then, Taghreed has joined me in a research project focused on foreign language anxiety and personality (Dewaele & Al-Saraj, to appear[1]), and became a Research Fellow in my department at Birkbeck, University of London. I admire her for her ability to overcome gender prejudice, for her adaptability, and for being funny, open-minded, and pragmatic, all while being a proud patriot.

Now, in this book, Taghreed provides a light-hearted exploration of foreign language anxiety, seen through the eyes of an active language learner who also happens to be a foreign language teacher and researcher. By blending personal experience with research, Taghreed highlights the strategies that both learners and teachers can use to manage students' anxiety levels, and to continue improving their skills in a new language.

Dr. Jean-Marc Dewaele

Professor
Birkbeck College
University of London

---

1. Dewaele, J.-M., & Al-Saraj, T. M. (Forthcoming). "Foreign Language Classroom Anxiety of Arab learners of English: The effect of personality, linguistic and sociobiographical variables." Name of Publication.

Note to My Readers

Nothing is more fantastic than learning a new language! The more languages you can learn, the better—imagine the people with whom you'll be able to communicate, not to mention the cultural exchanges that will take place.

The more we're able to interact across cultures, the better we'll understand other cultures, and the more tolerant and empathetic we'll be. Even though the world is getting smaller and more mobile, and we're close to a wealth of cultures, we're still very far from one another because of our lack of understanding.

By learning a language, you can help change that.

That's why anxiety should never prevent anyone from learning a language—the benefits are too great! It's also why I'm passionate about studying Foreign Language Anxiety, commonly abbreviated "FLA," and why I'm excited to inspire and empower you to overcome it.

In this book, I share a lot of what I learned through working on my doctoral thesis, *Exploring Foreign Language Anxiety in Saudi Arabia: A Study of Female English as a Foreign Language College Students*. It's my hope that students and teachers alike will benefit from my study.

Chapter One **1**

A Lifestyle of Learning

"Once you stop learning, you start dying." I've adopted this beautiful quote from Albert Einstein as one of my mottos in life.

I love learning. I get energized walking through college and university campuses. The idea of individuals being educated and enlightened—and therefore empowered to take charge of their destiny—makes my heart sing. As I write this, I'm living in California to conduct post-doctoral studies at the University of California, Berkeley—and I am the first Saudi Arabian woman to work as a post-doc at this university. When friends come to visit me, my idea of fun is to first give them a tour of the Berkeley campus, and then go to Stanford University. I want them to see what I see: Empowerment! I have the good fortune of being invited to give talks at universities all over the world, and when I do, I'm consumed by joy and happiness. I've visited some fine universities, including Waseda University in Japan, Harvard, Georgetown, Oxford, Yale, most of the University of London compasses, Cardiff University, Leeds Metropolitan University, Yıldız Technical University in Turkey, and probably a dozen more.

When it comes to a love for learning, my mother is my greatest role model. Although her marriage to my father was arranged when she was only 13 years old, she ultimately earned her university degree while raising a family of four children and running a busy household. She demonstrated the importance of education to me and my three siblings, and we took it seriously.

In Saudi Arabia in the 1960s and 1970s, it was common to marry very young. My father had joined the Royal Saudi Arabian Navy and was sent to Karachi University in Pakistan to study mechanical engineering. Halfway through his studies, he took a short break and went back to Saudi. While he was there, his brother-in-law—his sister's husband—suggested that he knew of the perfect bride for my dad. My dad and his brother-in-law went to see my grandfather together, to ask for my mom's hand in marriage. The day my dad asked for my mom's hand in marriage was also the day they met! My grandmother advised my mom that the groom, my father, had a bright future and would be a good husband. Upon meeting my dad, who also happened to be quite handsome, my mom agreed to the marriage. The wedding took place a week later, and then my dad went back to Pakistan with his new bride. His friends were shocked that he had gotten married while he was away on a weeklong break.

This scenario might seem shocking to Western readers, and it might even seem unpleasant. However, I believe much of the negativity tied to arranged marriages is due to misconceptions or stereotypes of how arranged marriages work. At least in Saudi, "arranged" doesn't always mean that a girl's parents choose her future husband. Sometimes a friend or family member makes a suggestion for a future wife or husband. Westerners tend to think that men and women whose marriages are arranged don't see one other until the wedding. That's a misconception. Not only do we see each other, but we have a say as to whether or not we want to marry the person.

Just a year after my mom was married, when she was only 14, I was born. She was alone a lot because Dad was in the navy and was often away on assignment for an extended period of time. To fill the gap, she spent time at the homes of Saudi friends who were living and studying in Pakistan. She enrolled in school with them—and fell in love with learning. My mother continued her studies when we went back to Saudi Arabia, and when it was time to study for exams, she sent me to stay with my grandparents in the western part of our country. I was still too young to attend school myself, and my grandmother took me everywhere with her. I particularly loved when we visited with her friends. The group of women sat in a circle, talking—and I sat on the side, listening.

We are each a product of our environment. My siblings and I grew up with learning all around us, so it's difficult for me to understand those who choose not to pursue their education. My mom is currently a high school principal. She is my inspiration, and has always told me, "Your education is your secret weapon."

I remember one time when I was very young, I told my father I didn't want to go to school because I didn't feel well.

"Are you dying?" he asked.

"No," I replied.

"Then you're going," he said in his military voice.

The importance of education was not to be questioned. Years later, the tables turned: I needed to have minor sinus surgery when I was a senior in high school. Early in the morning, my father brought me to the hospital and waited for me. When the surgery was over, he told me he was taking me home.

"Oh no! I can't go home … I have an exam in two days," I pleaded. "I need to go to school and get that lesson. I can't miss it."

"You're allowed to go back home after having surgery," replied my dad.

"No, please, just drop me off at school," I begged.

And so to school I went. After all, I wasn't dying. Besides, I intended to get perfect grades because I wanted to go into medicine, so I couldn't miss my class.

Perhaps by now you've realized I'm not the typical Saudi Arabian woman. Or, perhaps you don't know any other Saudi women but you recognize that I don't fit with the images portrayed by the media. I guess I've known since I was a child that I was a bit different. I realized that I wanted more from life than all my female friends, and that I see life very differently from how other Arab women see theirs. I was the firstborn in a Middle Eastern family, a female, and I had an innate need to prove to my parents that I could do as much as—and even more than—any boy could do. My father never expressed that he wanted a boy; yet, I wanted to prove to him he can count on me in everything. I am fortunate to have a dad who gave me the space and the freedom to be independent.

The typical Arab female is groomed for marriage from an early age. Growing up, I hated that! I was surrounded by friends who dreamed of the day they would marry and have kids. But not me. Those were not my dreams. I used to think to myself, "They'll never know what they're missing. I won't put my life on hold waiting for some guy." And wouldn't you know it? I was married at age 18. I didn't know my (then future) husband before he came to see me at my parents' home with the intent of marrying me. We call this "the seeing." My husband's father had passed away, so he brought his mother and older brother with him. We all sat down in the same room, and my husband and I saw each other for the first time! Neither of us was obligated to agree to marriage, but I guess each of us liked what we saw. We're both Western-educated and he has always encouraged my pursuit of education. Throughout our marriage, we've shared the value of education as well as pursued our educational goals and other dreams. We have three beautiful boys: our twins, Rayan and Kenan, and, Aban, our youngest.

There's a saying that we are our own worst enemy, and I am no exception. I've always pushed myself, sometimes to the brink, in order to succeed. Another one of my mottos is, "If you don't succeed once, try, try again!" If I fail at something, I look at how I can do it differently. There were times when I was ready to call it quits, throw in the towel and not complete my Ph.D. But, I knew I'd never forgive myself if I didn't pursue my dreams and I wanted to complete that research and earn that degree. I've driven myself to tears many times, wondering why I've pushed myself so hard. Only recently, I finally learned the answer to that question, when I was a participant in a life coach training program. Drive is linked to one's purpose, one's motivation. Helping others is my purpose, my fuel. It's my reason for getting out of bed every morning. Every once in a while, my husband poses the same question: "Why don't you just stay home, not work, take it easy—and have fun?" My answer to him? "I *am* having fun! Who says I am not having fun?" My motivation is probably different than most others', but aren't we all different (and special) in our own unique way?

Oh, don't get me wrong. I have girlfriends and I love going out with them. But that's not the most important thing to me, and my friends know it. "Taghreed is the problem solver," my girlfriends say about me. The role of problem solver is one I've played since I was a child, and it's one that brings me great joy. When I was as young as 13, whenever my mom, my siblings, and I were traveling to meet my dad—wherever he was stationed at the time—I would take it upon myself to take care of seating assignments and boarding passes at the ticket counter so my mother could stay with my younger siblings. I spoke fluent English at the time and was more outspoken than my mother. I had no problem communicating with the airline check-in people, whether in France, Pakistan, or the United States.

A few years later, our family spent two months driving across the United States. (Unlike me, my father loves the great outdoors and camping.) This was before the days of GPS, so each evening we'd plan the following day's route on a map. The next day, Dad would drive and I'd navigate. If we got lost, I was the one to ask for directions, a task I relished. I think having this sort of responsibility and freedom made me who I am: a fiercely independent woman who can do anything she sets her mind to.

I'm proud to say I've achieved success without compromising my Islamic religion and culture. I have never consumed alcohol nor have I smoked. I pray five times a day and fast during Ramadan (the holy month of fasting for Muslims), no matter where I am in the world. I can still be a devoted Muslim and a traditional Saudi female (a good wife and loving mother) while I conquer the world in my own way.

As a naval diplomat, my father was stationed in numerous countries around the world, so we moved frequently. I feel so fortunate to have had this experience, and I can only assume that the variety of experiences I had with my family in these countries helped me grow into the woman I am today. When I was only 7 years old, my family moved to Washington, D.C., in the United States. (I'll discuss this more in Chapter Three.) We moved back to Saudi Arabia when I was ready to enter secondary school. The differences in the classroom were a complete shock. Teaching—and learning—in Saudi Arabia was 180-degrees different from education in the United States. I was accustomed to classrooms in which questions were encouraged. In Saudi, students were subordinates: We were told what to do and when to do it. We listened and followed instructions. Interruptions were not allowed and there was absolutely no dialogue with the teacher. Imagine!

Needless to say, it didn't take long for me to become known among my classmates and teachers. I couldn't keep quiet. "She's no longer used to our culture," the teachers used to say about me. I'm happy to say they cut me some slack. They seemed to be impressed that I was fluent in English and they knew that would serve me well. My English skills were of little use in the Saudi classroom, however, except during my English lessons four times a week. I would still get swatted with a ruler on my palm for not following directions or for speaking in defense of my friends to prevent them from receiving the same punishment. I was and continue to be so outspoken that I could not—and cannot—watch something wrong or unjust occur in front of me while I do nothing. I am happy to report that this is no longer the case in the Saudi classroom as times have changed and new rules and regulations have been passed to protect students from physical punishment.

The traditional Saudi culture is very much about getting things right. When I was growing up, there was absolutely no "try, try again" attitude, although that has changed a little now. When I was in high school, each student had to take an exam twice a year, once at the end of each semester. If a student didn't pass an exam, they had to repeat the *entire* year. There was no such thing as a make-up test. Talk about pressure! (That was back in the 80s and 90s, and I'm happy to say that those particular, high-stakes exams have been abandoned.)

Memorization was the focus of many classes when I was in school in Saudi Arabia; there was a huge emphasis on rote learning. Unfortunately I had two things working against me: Since I had grown up in the U.S., I had become fluent in

English, and Arabic had become my second language; and, memorization was my greatest enemy. I was an excellent student with near-perfect grades in math, chemistry, and biology. I really struggled with literature and poetry because, of course, they were in Arabic and my Arabic wasn't that great. When it came time for exams in the literature course, students had to recite a poem or some other literary passage from memory. But, you didn't get to simply choose one poem and memorize it. You had to memorize many poems and then recite whichever one the teacher specified during a verbal exam! The teacher sat at a table in the front of the room with one or two chairs on the opposite side of the table. The students sat in their respective seats, waiting to be called by the teacher. There was not a sound in the room until the teacher called a student by name. When your name was called, you had to go to the front of the room, sit in front of the teacher, and recite whichever poem the teacher requested. The teacher had a pencil in her hand and was making notes about how well you were—or were not—doing. The majority of your final grade for the semester was based on how well you recited that single poem in front of the teacher, not to mention a classroom of peers anxiously rehearsing poems while awaiting their turns.

So there I was with my poor Arabic, having to regurgitate a poem I had attempted to memorize. I knew the material, but nonetheless, panic set in while I waited for my name to be next on the list. When my name was called, I slowly got up from my seat. I felt weak, saw dark spots in front of my eyes, and had heart palpitations. I thought I was going to be sick or faint. *What is wrong with me?* I wondered. *I've studied and I know this information.* But I couldn't talk any sense into myself, and I made mistakes in reciting a random poem chosen by the teacher. I knew the poem; it was there in my head, but I couldn't get it out. It got so bad that I finally went to my doctor.

"I can't take this anymore," I said to him. "At every exam, I get physically ill. I feel like I'm going to faint, and I can't breathe. Something is wrong with my breathing."

"Nothing is wrong with your breathing, Taghreed," he said. "You just need to calm down."

"Calm down?! How am I going to calm down? My entire grade depends on that one test."

My doctor handed me a prescription. "Take half of a pill before your exam and it will help with your anxiety."

Anxiety? That was a bad word in my mind. *A pill? I can't take a pill,* I thought to myself. Any kind of pill was a drug and I dislike taking any type of medication; but I finally realized I had no choice. Before my next exam, I took half of a pill. It made all the difference. I had no heart palpitations, no breathing problems—and I aced the test. This anxiety of mine would later become the motivation behind much of my work, and my aversion to the rote method would become my incentive for becoming a different type of teacher.

When I graduated from high school, my husband and I were married and moved to Miami to continue our educations. I learned I was pregnant just as I was finishing my associate degree. I decided to return to Saudi Arabia to have my twin baby boys—even though everyone thought I was crazy—as I was fearful of not having my mom nearby. She was a high school principal and couldn't take time off to come to the United States in the middle of the school year.

After the twins were born, my husband, our new babies, and I went back to Miami. My sister lived with us for a while, too, and she was also studying at the university in Miami. It was a struggle to juggle everything—life was a delicately balanced machine with many, many moving pieces! Through it all, my family supported me. My husband, sister, and I all worked together to take care of the twins. I finished my undergraduate degree and immediately started working on my master's degree. Meanwhile, I got a job working as a graduate assistant in the Department of Education at the University of Miami. In 2001, I got my master's degree and my husband got his second master's. We then moved back to Saudi.

In Saudi Arabia, I worked as a lecturer teaching English as a Foreign Language (EFL) and also devoted myself to community service. I helped organize fashion shows to benefit both kidney failure and cancer patients. In addition, I applied to the University of London for my Ph.D. I was drawn to the research of Dr. David Block, a professor there, and he would serve as my supervisor. Once I was accepted, the family and I moved to London, where we stayed until I completed my doctorate in 2011.

My youngest son, Aban, was born in 2005 while I was working on my Ph.D. I didn't feel that I was as involved with him as I was with the twins, and though I believe that was partially due to the fact London was not as child-friendly as Miami, it ate away at me. This guilt was yet another stressor on my shoulders.

As I worked toward my Ph.D. in the British system, the focus was on reading journals and books, and writing; there were no classes to take. I was always reading and writing, and felt guilty when I wasn't. Before falling asleep at night, I would lie down in bed, stare at the ceiling, and recap my day. *Did I do any writing today?* When the answer was "no," the guilt would creep up and snatch away any joy I'd experienced that day, whether while spending time with my family or while going out with friends for a much-needed change of scenery. I surely don't miss those days.

The day I passed my viva (the Ph.D. oral exam), I was on an emotional high as I walked home. It's something I will never forget. As soon as I walked in the door, I excitedly told my husband and the twins that I had defended my thesis and had barely a week's worth of corrections—that's very rare to receive in the British system and considered equivalent to highest honors.

"That's it for you? No more studying? So what are you going to do with your life now?" asked one of the twins.

"Now I have to get a life!" was my reply.

It was at that moment that I realized my sons saw me as a perpetual student. That was the only mom they knew. I believe my husband and I have been good examples to our children in demonstrating the importance of education. I also feel we have transferred our love of learning to them, although my youngest (now 10 years old) may not know it yet!

When I officially finished my Ph.D., I felt like I had to do something crazy to make the milestone memorable for me ... *but what?* I don't drink or smoke or go clubbing. Then, while on my daily walk, I passed a place called Claire's, which sells jewelry and similar accessories. In the back of the store, there it was: an ear-piercing corner! I'd found the outlet for my wild side. I'd always thought of getting a second hole in my ears, but was too much of a coward to do it. This was the time.

Getting my ears pierced was one of the craziest things I could have done since I was always taking care of others and being the responsible one. I was a role model for my boys, and I took my responsibilities very seriously! As was the case with earning my Ph.D., the process was painful, but the end result was joyful.

In 2014, I was accepted to the University of California, Berkeley as a Post-Doctorate Research Fellow. That's where I am as I write this book, and as I conduct further research on how language-related anxiety affects language learners from different cultures. I am really happy to be working at UC Berkeley, not only for myself, but also for my son Aban. He'd never had firsthand experience with the American educational system or culture, and I believe this exposure to another culture will benefit him a great deal, just as exposure to a variety of cultures impacted my perspective when I was growing up. It's amazing how kids adapt. After three months in the U.S., his British accent went out the window, and a laid-back California attitude emerged. I wrote some of this book while giggling to myself over my beloved 10-year-old son's overuse of the word "dude."

Chapter Two 2

My Saudi Arabia: Tradition and Transition

Oil and Development

Culture and Religion

Education

Saudi Women

Education and Employment for Saudi Women

Let's play a game. I'll say "Saudi Arabia," and you say … "Oil?" "Women covered in black with only their eyes showing?" "Camels?" "Terrorists?" Or, "Everyone's rich?"

When I was attending the University of Miami before September 11, 2001, and I told someone I was from Saudi Arabia, the typical response was, "Where's that?" I took great pride in explaining where my country is located: Saudi Arabia, an Arabic-speaking country of nearly 27 million people, is in southwestern Asia, occupying four-fifths of the Arabian Peninsula. The capital city is Riyadh. Saudi Arabia is bordered by the Arabian Gulf (known to the Arab countries as the Arabian Gulf) on the east and the Red Sea on the west, and shares borders with Iraq, Bahrain, Jordan, Egypt, the United Arab Emirates, Qatar, Oman, and Yemen. If my response resulted in a blank stare, I then said, "Saudi Arabia is just east of Egypt … It's on the eastern side of the Red Sea across from Egypt." Pretty much everyone knew that Egypt was in the eastern part of Africa, so that clarification seemed to suffice. Or sometimes I simply said, "Saudi Arabia is in the Middle East."

9/11 put Saudi Arabia on the map, but, unfortunately, not in a good way. Those in the West immediately began to associate Saudi Arabia with terrorists and terrorism. It was a major shift for me, to go from being from a country that wasn't known, to being from a country that was constantly in the media, but for all the wrong reasons. Yes, some of the 9/11 terrorists were from Saudi Arabia, but that doesn't mean everyone in Saudi is a terrorist, no more than every white person south of the Mason-Dixon Line is a member of the Ku Klux Klan.

My husband and I did—and still do—a lot of traveling back and forth to the United States and the United Kingdom from Saudi Arabia. After 9/11, we immediately felt the effects of traveling with a Saudi passport: The green cover quickly became known by the customs officials, and it often meant being sent to a room where we would have to sit for a minimum of four hours before being questioned about where we were going and the purpose of our trip. It wasn't easy, but I understood why we were questioned, and I wanted everyone to be safe. Before 9/11, as students at the University of Miami, we were able to secure our visas for travel to the United States in one day. After 9/11, the process became so long that on one occasion it took more than five months.

It saddens me to think of the reputation my country has earned across the globe because of the actions of a small number of people. We went from being non-existent in people's minds to not only existing, but being feared. Several months ago, I was sitting in on a graduate-level class on "Language and Identity" that was being taught by my colleague and mentor, Dr. Claire Kramsch. We were having discussions in groups of three; in my group, there were two Americans, a man and a woman. We began by introducing ourselves. I went last. When I said I was from Saudi Arabia, the guy sitting next to me turned as white as a ghost and sat straight up in his chair.

"From where?" he stuttered, a look of shock on his face.

I was startled, as was the other woman in our little group of three. I thought I'd done something wrong.

"I'm from Saudi Arabia," I repeated.

"Really?" he asked.

"Well, yes. Who would make up such a thing?" I responded.

"Wow, and you're okay? I mean, we hear things on the news about Saudi women …"

"I'm not sure what you hear, but yes, I'm fine. Here I am."

Finally, he seemed to let out a sigh of relief, and then he started laughing at himself. Like me, this man is an educated individual; he is working on his master's degree at UC Berkeley. Yet, he found himself highly influenced by the media.

This was proof to me that even though people in the West have heard of Saudi Arabia, they still know very little about it, and hold an (incorrect) stereotypical view of my country and its people. Most Westerners are shocked when I tell them that Saudi Arabia was only established in 1932. Its official name is the Kingdom of Saudi Arabia. As a country, we are still less than a century old. Think about it: The United States is 239 years old. England became a unified state in the 10th century. There are companies in the United States and the United Kingdom that are older than Saudi Arabia: Baker's Chocolate, an American company, is two-and-a-half-centuries old. The insurance company Lloyd's of London was founded in 1688.

A peaceful country, for years Saudi Arabia was like Switzerland: completely neutral. The only war in which we've ever taken part is the Gulf War in 1990 and 1991. When I think about the progress our country has made in less than a century, I'm very proud. We've essentially gone from being Bedouins in a country with very little infrastructure to being a thriving country that plays a unique role in the global energy industry.

Oil and Development

The Saudi economy was traditionally simple and dependent on pearl diving, date trading, camel exporting, and pilgrimage dues. However, Saudi Arabia has gained tremendous wealth in recent years due to the discovery of oil. In 1933, the King of Saudi Arabia gave permission to Standard Oil of California (SoCal), to prospect for oil, which was discovered in large quantities in 1938. The exporting of oil began a year later, though it was limited until after World War II. In the late 1940s, the Arabian American Oil Company (Aramco) was formed, with headquarters in Dhahran, on the east coast. By the 1970s, Saudi Arabia had become the top producer and exporter of oil in the world.[1] Thanks to the influx of oil investment money, the oil crisis of the 1970s, and the introduction of Western companies into Saudi Arabia to develop the infrastructure and maintain the oil supply, Saudis have gone from being Bedouins to being well-educated players on the global scene—in a single generation. According to the Saudi Arabian Ministry of Economy and Planning, Saudi Arabia now holds a quarter of the total Arab GDP and is the 25th largest importer/exporter in the world. This economic development has occurred against the backdrop of an extremely rigid, conservative, and traditional Islamic political system.

---

1.   Information Office of the Royal Embassy of Saudi Arabia in Washington, D. C. (2015). *About Saudi Arabia: Oil*. Retrieved from http://www.saudiembassy. net/about/country-information/energy/oil.aspx

With these economic changes came an influx of expatriates—from countries such as the United States, Britain, and Egypt—who arrived with modern, innovative ideas and contributed to the development of the country. Since 1990, there have been many changes. One example is the proliferation of television and media. Saudi Arabia has gone from having only two government TV channels and prohibiting TV satellites to having over 300 satellite channels broadcasting uncensored programs from all over the world.

Culture and Religion

Today, Saudi Arabia is divided into 13 regions, but from a cultural standpoint, there are three distinct areas: east, west, and central. I was born and raised in the west. Millions of pilgrims come from all over the world every year to visit the Two Holy Mosques in the west, one in Makkah and one in Madina. For those who follow the Islamic faith, Makkah and Madina are the two holiest cities on earth. Makkah was the birthplace of Islam and of the prophet Mohammad, and Madina is the location of the Prophet Mohammed Mosque as well as Mohammed's burial place. Those of us who live in this part of the country have more exposure to people from other countries who follow the Islamic faith and make the holy pilgrimage, so we tend be more exposed to different cultures than the rest of the country.

Saudi Arabia is an Islamic nation; state and religion are inseparable and closely intertwined with everyday life. Islam is the official, national religion and the tenets of Islam are enshrined as law. The political system of Saudi Arabia is based on a monarchy governed by the Shariah law, which is founded on Islamic policy. The Quran (the Holy book of Islam) serves as the basis of the constitution for the Kingdom. So, the laws in Saudi are based on the Quran, and everyone learns the Quran from a very young age, at home and in school. As Saudis, we accept and understand our laws and traditions (some of which are shocking to westerners) because they are part of our religion. However, ours is also culture steeped in tradition. There are laws that are not explicitly set out in the Quran. For example, women are not allowed to drive in Saudi Arabia, but the Quran certainly does not say that women cannot drive. In fact, there is no written law indicating that women are not allowed to drive—it's simply a cultural constraint.

Today fundamentalist groups such as ISIS and the Taliban manipulate and interpret our religion, (Islam), to serve their needs and justify their sick causes. As a result, many Westerners and non-Muslims have no understanding of what the Islamic faith is truly about. Our peaceful religion—which would never justify killing innocent human beings, no matter what faith they follow—has been given a bad name all over the world.

Education

Education throughout the Arab world—and Saudi Arabia in particular—has a history of being highly valued. There are separate schools for boys and girls, an accepted practice for our conservative Islamic society, and teachers command a high level of respect. Education is available to all citizens, though not mandatory by law. We have over 30,000 schools, 25 public universities, and 27 private universities.[2] According to a September, 2013 article in *The Economic Times,* the literacy rate in Saudi Arabia has increased from 40 percent in 1972 to 96 percent in 2013.[3]

Islam also shapes education in Saudi Arabia. Early schools in Saudi Arabia were called "katateeb" and reflected the centrality of religion in the culture in that only Islamic laws and basic literacy skills were taught. When Saudi Arabia became a country in 1932, education was available to boys only. Small groups of students, of varying ages, came together at a mosque to learn to read, and to memorize verses of the Quran. Education was regarded as a family matter, and the state was not involved. Today, Saudi Arabia has two authorities

2. Information Office of the Royal Embassy of Saudi Arabia in Washington, D. C. (2015). About Saudi Arabia: Education. Retrieved from http://www. saudiembassy.net/about/country-information/education/
3. Bennett, Coleman & Co. Ltd. (2013). Saudi Arabia's literacy rate reaches 96 per cent. *The Economic Times.* Retrieved from http://articles.economictimes. indiatimes.com/2013-09-12/news/42011621_1_literacy-rate-adult-education-night-schools

responsible for education policy and its implementation: The Ministry of Education and The Organization for Technical and Vocational Education.

As far as Saudi Arabia has come, there are drawbacks in the education system: Textbooks are developed, written, and published by the Ministry of Education, and issued to students for the students to keep. For years, the books were outdated, as they were republished annually without being updated in any way. The majority of teachers essentially walk their students through the textbooks, page by page, so students listen more than they participate. Exams, the only measure of students' success, are still all about memorization. This rigid system doesn't promote creative and independent thinking.

I'm happy to say that educational reform is beginning to take place, and it includes a decrease in the focus on rote learning. Today, curricula are being updated, and new teacher training programs are being implemented. However, the momentum pushing educational reform in Saudi Arabia is up against complex social and cultural challenges.

When I taught English in Saudi Arabia, I endeavored to be creative in my approach with students, instead of focusing simply on memorization. I tried to assign interesting projects as a way to get the students engaged with the English language, and not just focused on memorization. For example, I asked students to choose a destination for their "trip-of-a-lifetime vacation." They had to conduct research on the Internet, and then make a presentation to the class (in English, of course) about their dream destinations. I never viewed my students as my subordinates. I worked closely with them to help them succeed instead of taking the position of a superior teacher who stands in front of the class and demands memorization. I think it was a bit of a shock for my students at first as I was essentially using a Western approach to teaching. They came to look forward to my classes, however, and even told me how much they enjoyed them.

One of Saudi Arabia's most ambitious strategic plans is to send Saudi Arabian youth to the West to complete their higher education. These students gain the necessary experience and knowledge to participate in the development of the country and improve international relations when they return to Saudi. To that end, in the 1970s, the government began providing scholarships for students to study abroad, and wealthier Saudi families also sent their children abroad to further their kids' education. The process of sending students abroad has continued and increased through the years.

Saudi Arabian students who have studied in the West often return home with a desire to improve and change social, technological, and educational standards and systems in their home country. Their desire and ambition has resulted in a conflict between adapting to change and preserving traditional culture. One example is women being allowed to drive. The majority of Saudis who support women driving are members of the younger generation who were educated in the West. As students they saw women driving regularly, and may have even driven themselves; but when they returned to Saudi Arabia, those who were women couldn't drive! Most who oppose women's right to drive cannot accept the wave of change that is coming to the country, like it or not. This wave of change is non-threatening, except to traditions, and has nothing to do with religion.

In addition, private, English medium universities (those where English is the primary language used for teaching every subject) are attempting to move away from rote learning to a more interactive style of education. There, students are encouraged to ask questions and participate in projects that require them to gather information beyond that which is presented in textbooks. English medium universities are relatively progressive, with modern teaching methods that are significantly different than those used in the Saudi public educational system. First established in Saudi Arabia in the late 1990s, the private education sector has expanded rapidly, and women represent a growing number of students. These English medium institutions implement American models of education and administration, and all classes are held in English. While men and women still study separately, these schools provide Western-influenced social environments, from the extracurricular activities these schools offer (e.g., debate, physical education and sport teams, student government, and student clubs) to the Western-style clothing and hairstyles of the students.

To be accepted into one of these private, English medium universities, students must obtain a minimum score on a test that measures English ability, or successfully pass the English as a Foreign Language (EFL) program offered by the university where they want to study. While each of these EFL programs is different, all teach a level of English beyond what students learn in secondary school, and all use interactive methods of education that are uncharted territory for students who are accustomed to traditional, rote learning methods. For example, in the EFL program in which I taught, students took classes in reading and writing, listening and speaking, and grammar, and were required to perform in a Western environment that uses a Western style of teaching. As I'll share in the chapters to come, the unfamiliar learning environment of these EFL programs plays a big role in foreign language anxiety (FLA).

Saudi Women

For the most part, I believe Westerners have a stereotypical view of Saudi women as being oppressed, and I can understand why. Women's rights, which are defined by our government, are changing—albeit slowly—not unlike the way women's rights have evolved in other countries. To put things in perspective, compare the evolution of women's rights in Saudi Arabia to the history of women's voting rights in the United States. When the United States was founded in 1776, only landowners were allowed to vote. Eighty years later, in 1856, voting rights were expanded to all white men. Fourteen years after that, the 15th amendment was passed, stating the right to vote could not be denied based on race. It wasn't until 1920, when the United States was 144 years old, that the right to vote was expanded to women.[4] Relatively speaking, Saudi Arabia extended this right decades earlier: In 2011, the King declared that women could both vote and run for office in local elections, just 79 years into its history as a nation.[5]

Many people in the Western world know that women are not allowed to drive in Saudi Arabia. This is true, and it's an inconvenience. Am I in favor of women driving? Absolutely!

---

4. Constitution of the United States, Amendment XIX. Retrieved from http://www.archives.gov/exhibits/charters /constitution_amendment_19.html
5. Information Office of the Royal Embassy of Saudi Arabia in Washington, D. C. (2014). *Saudi Women to Vote and Run in Municipal Council Elections*. Retrieved from http://www.saudiembassy.net/press-releases/press 07241401.aspx

Saudi women want to drive and in the last few years, they have waged many campaigns in hopes of being able to drive. I do believe it will happen eventually. I had the opportunity to be in the presence of King Abdullah when he was Crown Prince, a little more than a decade ago. I was with a group of women and we heard him say, "I await the day that these parking lots are not filled with drivers, but our culture is still not ready. Have patience." I was reassured that the King was not against women driving. I write about this memory with a heavy heart, because just recently, King Abdullah passed away. However, I remember King Abdullah with joy and appreciation for all he did for our country—even when he was nearly 80, he was forward-thinking! It saddens me that King Abdullah never saw the day when women could drive in Saudi Arabia, but I also have great hope that our new leader King Salman, will see this change materialize soon.

Remember, culture and religion are one and the same in Saudi, so it goes back to our very traditional culture, and the Saudi clerics who are against women driving. There are, however, Bedouin women who drive out of necessity: Bedouins live a nomadic lifestyle in the desert in the central part of Saudi Arabia, and Bedouin women often drive pickup trucks to help their husbands gather their sheep. But, there are no police officers or clerics in the desert to stop them or enforce the cultural norms prevalent in the less-isolated regions of Saudi Arabia.

When women are finally allowed to get behind the wheel, regulations will be needed to protect them. For example, female police officers (currently none exist in Saudi Arabia) must be hired and trained, in order to interact with women drivers when it's necessary for the law to get involved. Islam dictates that women should not have physical contact with men except for male relatives—our fathers, brothers, husbands, sons, and uncles. It would not be acceptable for an unfamiliar man—even a police officer—to arrest a woman, or even to stop a woman on the highway. Her male guardian must be present for any interaction with a man from outside the family. So, unless we have female police officers, it will be culturally unacceptable to enforce driving laws upon female drivers. In addition, due to the necessity of separating men and women, holding cells (in prisons) must be designated specifically for women. There are all-female prisons and prison guards in Saudi Arabia, despite the fact that the crime rate is very low, particularly among women. However, without short-term or temporary holding cells for women only, it would be unacceptable to arrest female drivers.

In my mind, there are additional laws and regulations I would like to see changed that are just as important, if not more important, as women being able to drive: One is the male guardianship system. When women travel or leave the country, they must be accompanied by a male guardian, or be given written permission to travel outside the country. If a woman is not married, her father is her guardian. If she is married, then her husband is her guardian. Women also need their guardian's permission to open a bank account in Saudi Arabia. My first bank account was in the United States. When I went to open a bank account for the first time in Saudi Arabia, I was given papers to sign. As I was signing the papers one by one, I came across a form that indicated I had to get my husband's permission to open an account. It was a bit of a shock to me, but not a big deal. I took the paper to my husband, he signed it, we laughed about it, and I submitted the signed documents to the bank.

However, this small incident, which was merely an inconvenience for me, prompted me to think about the implications of requiring a male guardian's permission. What if a woman is trying to save money for herself and doesn't want her husband to know? What if her guardian isn't trustworthy and she isn't comfortable sharing what she does with the funds she's earned? Since we don't pay income taxes in Saudi Arabia, we don't need to declare our earnings to the government, yet women must disclose their financial intentions to their husbands or legal guardians, even if it is just to open a bank account. That doesn't seem right to me, nor does it make any sense. I want women to be able to own businesses and to open bank accounts—on their own, without the permission of a guardian. I am not happy with the speed of change when it comes to women's rights in Saudi, but this process involves changing perceptions and pre-conceived beliefs, which are among the most difficult things to change. On the bright side, change is coming even as I write this.

I believe Westerners have another stereotypical view of Saudi women—that we are always covered in plain black, from head to toe, with only our eyes revealed. The black, full-body covering is called "abaya"; it is a loose over-garment that covers everything except the face, feet, and hands. The purpose of the abaya is to shift attention away from the physical shape of the body by covering up while in public. Underneath the abaya, a woman can wear anything she chooses. When she goes to a friend's house, a woman can take off the abaya, as it is not typically worn among friends or family. The face covering, or face veil, that leaves only the eyes showing is called the "burqa" or "niqāb." However, it isn't mandatory that we cover our faces, and not all women do. Islam requires only that we cover our hair, but some choose to cover their faces as well. The exact manner in which a woman covers up depends on how religious she is, as well as her personal preference and family upbringing.

We've come a long way since the basic black abaya. There was a time when the basic black abaya was ubiquitous, the go-to outer garment to wear. It was the Little Black Dress of Saudi women's culture! It made dressing simple, and a woman always felt secure she had the right thing to wear. Nowadays, there are different styles of abayas: abayas for running errands, abayas for shopping or meeting a friend for coffee, and abayas for work. Abayas are becoming very fashionable. Those for parties and weddings are very elaborate with intricate details of colorful lace and rhinestones. The younger generation is making a statement with their abayas. I've even seen teenagers wearing denim abayas.

When I travel to the more traditional, central part of our country, or the capital (Riyadh), I wear a plain black abaya—it's still the go-to abaya—because the atmosphere in the capital is more conservative, at least in my perspective. But, if I'm visiting a girlfriend, I'll wear a more fashionable abaya. In my view, Saudi women wearing abayas can be compared to the Amish wearing their simple clothing: It's part of their culture. Wearing an abaya is tradition and religion, but not mandatory. It's actually not against the law to go out without an abaya. However, if a woman goes out without an abaya, she could be approached by the religious police (called the "motawa'ah") and asked why she is not covered up, or asked to cover up. Wearing an abaya may seem strange to women in the West. However, I have a lot of friends who are expats—Americans, Brits, Lebanese, Syrians, and Egyptians—working in Saudi, and when they travel outside of the country they often say to me that life would be easier if they just always wore their abayas. It's so convenient, the pressure to choose just the right outfit is removed, and no one knows what you're wearing underneath!

Education and Employment for Saudi Women

According to a March, 2014 article in *Yale Global Online*,[6] female students in Saudi Arabia now outnumber male students at the university level. Women's education is now regarded positively in that it is seen as enabling women to do their part to fulfill the social and economic requirements of the country, and all women are encouraged to complete their undergraduate education.

Whereas women used to get married very young (in their teenage years), now women are marrying after they graduate from college, and many women do not marry until they are in their mid-20s and 30s. I've seen many women finish their undergraduate degree and go on to pursue a master's degree because they're not married and are not yet qualified for a job they want. They don't want to sit at home without something meaningful to do. Saudi society is also beginning to recognize that women, not just men, have the potential to play a valuable part in advancing the country and its economy.

In the past, many Saudi women went through the educational system all the way through university, but stayed home instead of actively using their educations. In part, this trend was due to the historical belief in Saudi Arabia (and in the West not so long ago) that a woman worked only if her husband or parents did not have enough money to provide for her. A woman working could bring shame to a husband or family, implying that the husband (or father) was an inadequate provider. Today, it no longer matters if a Saudi woman's family is rich or poor. Women from all backgrounds choose to work. Yes, it may be the case that a woman works because her family benefits from her income;

6. Chamie, J. (2014). Women more educated than men but still paid less. *Yale Global Online*. Retrieved from http://yaleglobal.yale.edu/content/women-more-educated-men-still-paid-less-men

however, it is no longer assumed that a woman who works does so only out of necessity. Women are gaining the freedom of choice. Some women choose to stay home to raise their children, and work outside of the home later. Others feel a great sense of accomplishment from developing careers, earning money, and giving back to their communities by working. To me, the most important thing is that a woman is able to make choices, and I'm thrilled that Saudi women have that ability. I cannot say how much I value the fact that I myself have had the freedom to choose to pursue education and to work outside the home.

While I always encourage women to pursue their degrees if that's their choice, I recognize that what I value deeply is not necessarily the same as what others value: Some of my peers couldn't wait to finish their degrees, get married, and stay home. Others dropped out of college as soon as they got married. I can't comprehend that, but it's not my place to decide how they spend their lives. Sometimes our differences make us more beautiful than our similarities, and I've learned to accept that not every Saudi woman has education at the top of her agenda like my mother and me.

Saudi Arabia has also enjoyed advancement in the types of jobs women hold. English medium universities are opening new fields of study to women as these institutions offer majors and courses in areas such as graphic design, interior design, engineering, and finance to female students. These schools also allow Saudi women to obtain a Western standard of education, even if their families are opposed to them traveling abroad to study. Historical restrictions on women's jobs were based on social traditions and customs that have been upheld for centuries in Saudi Arabia. Islam itself does not restrict the opportunities women may be given; the restrictions that are in place are the result of individuals' beliefs. The majority of working women used to be teachers. That was the hot thing to be because teachers start the workday early and are home by mid-afternoon, in time to cook dinner and to be home when the head of the house arrives. Plus, teaching positions were the highest-paying jobs for women, though that is no longer the case.

Keep in mind that women and men are segregated in education (as in most everything), so there was and is a need for female teachers to teach female students. As of 2013, the Saudi government has permitted women to obtain licenses to practice law. Female lawyers now deal with women's issues, such as divorce and child custody. Prior to this, women with legal degrees were only allowed to be legal consultants, and as such they couldn't work with or represent clients inside courtrooms. And, we now have female engineers and many more female doctors than we used to. Historically, medicine was seen as a profession that required a non-segregated environment. Nowadays, women can train to work in health care, but only the most liberal or forward-thinking parents (or husbands) allow their daughters (or wives) to enter medical professions.

While some things advance, some things stay the same: At the college or university level, certain fields of study, such as flight engineering or mechanical engineering, aren't even offered to women. These fields are considered inappropriate areas for women's education or employment. These professions are heavily reliant on men, and so a woman would be unable to find a position in these fields, as companies do not offer positions that are segregated from men. To be fair, I don't think many Saudi females are interested in these fields, nor do I think these would be appropriate professions for women in Saudi Arabia, given that these fields are dominated by men.

Just as it's important to recognize the degree of progress that has been made in Saudi Arabia, it's important to acknowledge that while women in the West (in countries such as the United States) are allowed to earn degrees in fields like engineering, women in those fields are still in the minority and they face challenges in getting jobs. As a part of an entrepreneurship course I'm taking at the Berkeley Haas School of Business, I interviewed a female entrepreneur who is a structural engineer in San Francisco. She mentioned that when she was in college in the 1980s, she was the only female in her engineering program. When it came time for her to get a job, she was the only female candidate competing with 40 males for one position in a company. She identified gender bias as an issue in her field, both then and now. So, you see, these issues are present in both young countries like Saudi Arabia, and in older, more developed countries, like the United States. In both countries' cultures, progress is being made toward respecting the rights of both men and women, though progress is measured differently in each culture. I don't think it's fair to judge either culture or country by the standards of the other.

The education of women in Saudi Arabia has brought about innovative changes in a variety of sectors of Saudi Arabian society, including the appointment of the first female Deputy Minister of Education in February of 2009. This is the most senior role ever held by a woman in the Kingdom of Saudi Arabia. These changes promise to offer greater participation for women in education and employment, as well as allowing women greater participation and rights in the public sphere.

I dislike Western media's portrayal of Saudi Arabia, and Saudi women in particular. Many in the West tend to focus on the restrictions and problems, and they miss the fact that under the surface, transformation is taking place, some of it led by educated women.

We have made incredible progress for a country that is less than a century old. Please don't expect us to be at the same level as the United States or a European country. Tradition is changing.

Views are changing. The country is changing for the better. But change is difficult, particularly when it comes to changing a way of life that has been in existence for centuries. I consider this to be the most challenging type of progress. We must remember that change is always faced with resistance, but determination will help to see the change through.

Chapter Three **3**

My Journey as a Language Learner

"Et cetera, et cetera, et cetera."

For some, these words might bring back memories of Yul Brynner in *The King and I.* But to me, they were my motivation to learn English.

My family came to the United States in the 1980s, when I was 7 years old. I knew only two English phrases: "How are you?" and "My name is Taghreed," and one additional English word: "business." I'd learned those phrases because we'd been living at the naval base in Jeddah, Saudi Arabia, where my dad was stationed, and we had numerous Western visitors, all of whom spoke English. (I really don't know why I knew the word "business," other than I picked it up while living on the naval base, and I liked the sound of it.)

Imagine for a moment that you're sent to a foreign country. The country is very different from yours, yet beautiful, and you're over the moon with excitement about this adventure. You don't know the language other than to say, "My name is …" and "How are you?" When you arrive, you're overwhelmed with the sights and sounds of this unfamiliar country, but desperate to soak it all in. You know that to really experience this place, you need to interact with its people, but there's one problem—you don't understand a word they're saying! You'd love to make a few local friends, but how can you if you can't communicate with anyone? That was me.

I was sent to a standard American elementary school, and placed in an ordinary class—as opposed to an ESL (English as a Second Language) program. I understood nothing. I dutifully sat in my chair, listened, and observed. Of course, I never volunteered to answer the teacher's questions, because I had no idea what she was saying or asking. This went on for days. I was silent, and that was very unlike me.

One morning, the teacher wrote something on the blackboard. I was in my usual seat, staring down at my desk. Then the teacher turned back to the class and said, "Et cetera, et cetera, et cetera."

What was that? I thought.

And then, without even knowing what I was doing, I blurted out, "Et cetera, et cetera, et cetera."

The teacher stopped what was she was doing to look at me, and the entire class burst out in laughter. And then I realized I hadn't said "Et cetera, et cetera, et cetera" in my head, but out loud. I just loved the intonation in those words, even though I had no idea what they meant. I laughed right along with everyone else, but deep inside I wasn't happy because I felt I was being made fun of. Saving face is an important aspect of the Saudi culture and I decided right then and there that I would never be laughed at again because of my inability to speak English: I would learn this new language. It was a turning point for me.

Another motivating factor for me to learn English was my need to understand the other kids. Although I played with them outside during recess, I didn't always know what they were saying; but, I wanted to. And, like all kids, I loved watching television—especially cartoons—and I wanted to understand everything that was going on. My favorite shows were *Superman* and *Wonder Woman* as superheroes captured my imagination. When I watched these programs, I was able to connect what the characters were doing with what they were saying, and it helped me with my English. I also enjoyed watching comedy shows, as we had nothing like them in Saudi Arabia: I'd tune in to *Charlie's Angels* and *CHIPS*, and sometimes *Three's Company*, *Happy Days*, and *The Facts of Life*—basically anything that was on TV before 7 p.m. Even though I didn't know it at the time, I think these shows, more than the others, helped me better understand American culture as I was able to pick up on what was considered funny or embarrassing. I was especially fascinated that there were three female detectives in *Charlie's Angels*! *There is nothing women can't do*, I thought to myself. We can find the bad guys and still look great!

From those TV shows, I learned to laugh at my mistakes with others, and that it's even alright to make fun of yourself. Most of these shows were comedy shows, so they were light-hearted and filled with (often silly) humor. Looking back, I find it funny how I, as a child, picked up all these hidden messages and started to adapt, accept the cultural norms, and use what I learned from TV in daily life. I would say, "oh well ..." and continue on in any situation, whether it was being unable to pronounce a word correctly, speaking my mind about an important issue, having the courage to ask a question, or stating that I liked or disliked something.

Between attending school, playing with my new friends, and watching television, I was speaking English in three months. When we had American guests come to our home, I always spoke English with them, and they would invariably compliment me, saying, "Your English is excellent. You don't even have an accent." Accolades are a great motivator for a 7-year-old. I became even more diligent in the pronunciation of my American English and asked my teacher and friends for help whenever I wasn't sure of a word.

It's easier to learn a foreign language when you're immersed in it, and children learn foreign languages more readily than adults. Their brains are more able to take in the language; their mouths are more able to reproduce the correct sounds. And, very young children have no anxiety about making mistakes. When my husband and I attended the University of Miami, all of our friends were Hispanic. The adults in the neighborhood used to sit outside and chat while all of our kids played together. Before we knew it, our twin boys were able to understand Spanish, and then they started to pick up words here and there. Children naturally want to interact with one another, and that becomes their motivation. Our kids wanted to blend in and play with the Spanish-speaking kids, so they were motivated to learn a new language, knowingly or not.

My Decision to Learn Turkish

There's a large Arab community in London, and when I lived there, I always enjoyed getting together with my friends. They're an eclectic group. Some of them are well-educated while others married very young and never pursued higher education. One thing we all have in common is that we love to have a good time. A couple of years ago, whenever I was at any Arab gathering, the topic of conversation inevitably turned to soap operas— specifically, Turkish soap operas. The situation was the same when I would visit my hometown, Makkah, or Jeddah in Saudi Arabia. *A soap opera? Are you kidding? I don't have time to watch television!* I dismissed these Turkish television dramas as complete and total silliness, but talk of what was happening on one specific drama series was never-ending. Intrigued by my friends' passion and emotion about this program, I felt that same drive I'd experienced as a child when I simply had to know what the other kids were talking about. I decided I had to see for myself what these soaps were all about.

I watched two episodes—dubbed in Arabic—of the famous drama series entitled *Fatmagül'ün Suçu Ne?* ("What is Fatmagül's fault?"). As a researcher and an inherently curious person, I wanted to know the complete plot so I could get a full understanding of what was happening, and I learned that this series was based on real events that took place back in the 1970s. Specifically, it told of a rapist who'd been allowed to marry the rape victim in order to escape prison and punishment, due to a flaw in the Turkish law at the time. It also showed how the rape victim found the courage to take her case to court and won, and how the Turkish law regarding punishment of rape was changed. As a woman, this story intrigued me.

As I continued to search the Internet for more episodes of *Fatmagül'ün Suçu Ne?,* I found that a variety of TV shows are often an inspiration for Arab women in many ways, not the least of which is that these shows encourage women to speak out. In fact, these TV programs are so popular in the Arab world that during the Palestinian Civil War between Hamas and Fatah, the two sides agreed to a one-hour ceasefire at 4 o'clock in the afternoon—because they were watching a Turkish TV series![1] I was shocked to learn that, but it was true and the soldiers were not ashamed to admit it during a TV interview. Moreover, these

---

1. Sevim, N. (2012). Turkish TV – a device for social change in the Arab world? Euronews. Retrieved from http://www.euronews.com/2012/06/29/turkish-tv-a-device-for-social-change-in-the-arab-world/

Turkish TV drama series were popular because they showed Arab viewers that Western lifestyles can co-exist with Islamic and Arab identities and culture.

The impact that these popular Turkish TV dramas have had in Saudi Arabia has not always been positive, however. The most famous Turkish TV drama to hit the Arab world, "Gümüs," was one of the first shows to be dubbed into Arabic; it was a huge sensation in Saudi Arabia and the Middle East, with 95 million viewers.[2] It couldn't have hurt that the male lead was incredibly handsome, and particularly appealing to Arab women! The heartthrob's real name is Kıvanç Tatlıtuğ, but he is famous in the Arab world as "Mohannad," the role he portrayed on television. When the series was airing, parents all throughout the Arab world named their newborn boys Mohannad. Women had arguments with their husbands (and some got divorced!) because the men were so upset that their wives were falling in love with "Mohannad" on TV. I thought it was just a fad, but since then, women have swooned over other leading men from Turkish TV drama series. Even now, traveling to Turkey is popular among Middle Eastern tourists due in part to the popularity of this (and other) TV dramas, a testimony to the power of the media and its influence on individuals.

---

2. Paschalidou, M. N. (2014). Aljazeera TV- Kismet: *How Soap Operas Changed the World*. Retrieved from http://www.aljazeera.com/programmes/witness/2013/11/kismet-how-soap-operas-changed-world-20131117152457476872.html

So, I found myself hooked on *Fatmagül*, and I could hardly wait to see what happened next. However, the dubbed version of the program was delayed by a couple of weeks because of the time it took to translate it from Turkish to Arabic and then to dub it. I didn't want to wait—why couldn't I just watch the Turkish version? There was just one small problem: I didn't understand Turkish. I searched the Internet, found a website that aired the episodes sooner than they were dubbed and aired on Arabic television channels, and began watching the series online. Then an odd thing happened: With each episode that I watched, I became more attuned to the Turkish, and started to pick up the similarities between Turkish and Arabic. Then something else happened: The language in the TV program reminded me of my grandparents. The holy city of Makkah, where I was born, had a Turkish influence, as that area of the country was once occupied by the Turkish Ottoman Empire. I remembered the days when I sat listening to my grandmother's circle of friends: I heard them use some words that are no longer used in colloquial Arabic today, but are part of the Turkish language. I felt joy when I heard these words in *Fatmagül,* as they called to mind memories of happy days with my grandparents. I actually knew what these words meant. I decided right then and there that I had to learn Turkish.

As I reflect on my experience with the TV drama series, I understand my motivation for wanting to learn Turkish: I was hooked on the story and watching it in Turkish gave me both enjoyment and the satisfaction of learning. Watching the series brought back wonderful childhood memories of my grandparents. And, I enjoyed seeing the similarities between the Turkish and Arabic cultures, as well as between the Turkish language and *Makkawi* (an old Arabic dialect spoken mainly in Makkah). Each of us has our motivation for wanting to learn something new, and an individual's motivation doesn't need to make sense to anyone else. Your motivation as a language learner only needs to resonate with you.

As a language anxiety researcher, I wondered if I would experience the same anxiety that my students dealt with when they were learning English in Saudi Arabia. In a way, I thought I'd be able to avoid these feelings since I knew what makes language students anxious. While teaching and then working on the Ph.D., I spent many of my days, and sometimes nights, aware of and thinking intellectually about the experience of language-related anxiety. Surely, this hyper-awareness would make me immune to experiencing this anxiety. Of course, should even a trace of anxiety appear, I would simply apply the techniques I knew to reduce it. I had given numerous presentations on recognizing and reducing this anxiety. I'm an expert! As a researcher, this would be a fun little experiment. I'd use myself as a guinea pig to test my ideas, and to see if I, too, would experience language learning anxiety even though

I am a researcher in the field.

My Turkish language learning journey started in February of 2013. I researched where I could learn Turkish and was informed that the Cultural Center in London provides classes at many levels. I signed up as soon as I learned of this opportunity, happy to start the journey. To be honest, I thought I was ahead in the process since I was already watching the Turkish TV drama and had some Turkish words under my belt.

After several months of study, I decided to visit Turkey on my way to Saudi Arabia to try out my Turkish. After attempting a single sentence, I suddenly realized what my language students and the students in my doctoral thesis studies had been telling me all along. I was in the Grand Bazaar in Istanbul trying to buy a set of Turkish coffee cups. Previously, I had seen a specific design, and I wanted *that* design. I was determined to return to London (where I was living at the time) with the set I loved, so I had no choice but to try to communicate to the merchant the type I wanted. I tried and tried to describe the design, but I couldn't get my sentence out! It was there—in my head— and it was perfect. But I couldn't say it. As I've mentioned, my Arabic culture doesn't have a "try, try again" philosophy. We must get it right, or not say it at all. But I did try, try again. Finally, I took a couple of deep breaths and then my Western influence took charge: I gave it a try, interspersing English words and using hand gestures to help clarify what I was trying

73

to say. When the Turkish merchant finally understood what I was attempting to communicate, he went back to his storage center and came back with the very set I was looking for. I was over the moon. It had worked—I had spoken in Turkish, communicated, and gotten what I wanted. What a boost to my morale and motivation! I started thinking to myself that I wasn't that bad in Turkish, evidence of the mentality I had probably picked up from the American comedy shows. So what if I'd looked funny? When all was said and done, I'd gotten my message across.

I Have Language Anxiety!

When I arrived at Berkeley, I had been studying Turkish for about 10 months, and I decided to continue my study of Turkish by auditing a class. I found a professor who was teaching Level II Turkish and enrolled even though the students were more advanced than I. Auditing a course requires full participation in the class, possibly including taking exams (though that is up to the student and professor to decide), but the student does not earn a formal grade or credit toward a degree. At the beginning of the third week of class, the professor announced there would be an exam on Friday. I, the language expert, went into panic mode.

The morning of the test, I woke up at 4 a.m. so I could spend some additional time studying. This wasn't my long-term study plan; I couldn't sleep and I felt like I needed to cram for the test. Panic set in again. I simply didn't want to take the Turkish exam. I finally got dressed. "Just another 10 minutes," I heard a little voice inside me say. "Just another 10 minutes." I heard it again. I finally walked outside to my car—in slow motion. I drove to the campus, parked, and walked to the classroom where I found all the other students already taking the test. I had gotten up at 4 o'clock in the morning and I was late! The teacher handed me the exam and I went to an empty seat. I looked down at the exam and didn't understand a thing. Not a single word—it was as if the test had been written in Chinese characters. I blanked out completely. *What happened to all the time I spent studying Turkish? This can't be happening to me.* When the professor let us know that the allotted time for the exam was over, everyone handed in their tests and we continued with our regular class. Everyone except me, that is. I pretended to listen, but I was still in shock, trying to process what had happened to me over the last several hours since I had gotten out of bed. But my head was spinning. At the conclusion of the class, I tried to sneak out the door.

"Are you giving me your test?" the professor asked.

"It's okay. I didn't get to finish it," I replied with one foot out the door, and I scurried out.

When I returned home, I pulled the test out of my briefcase. I looked at it in amazement—because I more or less understood everything on it. And then it hit me: I had anxiety, too, just like the students in my research in Saudi Arabia. I had cracked under the pressure of the exam and my need to do well. I spent the rest of the afternoon reflecting on my conversations with the Saudi students with whom I'd worked so closely while conducting research for my doctoral thesis. I'd never really understood what they were saying until that moment. I certainly had empathy for them, but until I experienced this anxiety myself, I never fully understood what they had been saying. The students said they "couldn't understand" English, as if the teacher were suddenly speaking in a made-up language or Chinese, even though the students had studied English for years. Now, I knew that feeling. I had not fully understood when they said they "just couldn't do it," or when they simply failed to come to class on time. Now, I was seeing those things in myself, but only after the fact.

No One Is Exempt

I thought about my experience at the Turkish Cultural Center in London, where I had begun studying Turkish. It wasn't an academic environment, which meant there was no pressure to perform well on an exam. Even though I knew the material, the idea of having to take an exam made my stomach whirl and my brain go blank.

And then I realized it wasn't only the test. At the cultural center, the Turkish teacher always attempted to engage the students in conversation by having us answer questions at the end of each chapter in the textbook. In other words, we had to speak out loud in front of our fellow students. The teacher always went around the room and called on individual students based on where we were sitting. I used to get increasingly nervous as my turn approached. I scurried to figure out which question would be mine and tried to practice my answer in my head. I was so nervous about it that as I look back on it now, I realize I didn't really enjoy the class all that much even though the teacher was fantastic and had a great sense of humor with us students. Lots of questions flooded my mind: *Why is it so important to get it right? Why am I mainly practicing my answer instead of paying attention to the other students' answers? Why not just go with the flow and see what comes out of me when it's my turn? Is it competitiveness or is it anxiety? Or, a bit of both?*

Over and over, my mind would flash back to what my research participants told me about their anxiety in language class. I knew most of *their* anxiety stemmed from the teacher (more on that in Chapter Seven), but that wasn't the issue in my case. My teacher was engaging and supportive. She did not have favorites, nor did she treat her students as subordinates. We were actually praised for learning Turkish—the teacher was very happy to see all her students learning the Turkish language.

My personal experience has taught me that none of us is exempt from language anxiety, not even a language anxiety researcher.

As a public speaker, I often address groups of 50 or more. I may have those first few butterflies in my stomach—even veteran speakers get butterflies—but I never experience anxiety over speaking. I'm confident and passionate about my subject matter. But I knew I'd experienced this type of anxiety in the past, and realized the Turkish exam at UC Berkeley and having to speak out loud at the cultural center in London weren't the only times I had gotten queasy when it came to a foreign language: I thought back to my struggle to memorize and recite Arabic poems while in high school in Saudi Arabia. When I had returned to Saudi Arabia after spending several years in the United States, Arabic was no longer my dominant language. My Arabic had become rusty, and when I had to memorize and take tests in Arabic, I was very anxious. I'd always wondered how others could feel so calm while taking exams, but it had never occurred to me that my anxiety wasn't simply an unavoidable part of the learning process.

I am an anxious language learner. I believe that subconsciously I'd known this all along, but had refused to recognize it until I reflected on my Turkish language learning experience.

Chapter Four 4

From Frustration to Exploration

As I came to see myself as an anxious language learner, I began to see my experiences as an English teacher in Saudi Arabia in a new light. One student in particular stood out in my mind: Amina.

On a single Saturday morning in a listening and speaking class that I taught, Amina had already provided what seemed like a month's worth of distractions. Not only did her constant outbursts steal the attention of the class, she completely disregarded my requests to speak only in English while in class, and told stories completely irrelevant to the lesson. With just four students in the class, it was hard for anyone in the classroom to ignore Amina's disruptions.

I tried encouraging Amina. I tried engaging her. I tried the rational approach, reminding her that learning a new language as an adult is somewhat like learning language as a small child, and that mistakes are a part of the learning process. But, despite my best efforts, I couldn't curb her behavior—or its effect on the entire class. I was exasperated.

I wasn't alone in my frustration. When I asked some of my fellow foreign language teachers about Amina's behavior in class, I learned that she was disruptive in their classrooms as well. I speculated about what problems she might be having and why she might be acting out in this way, but was stumped.

In the meantime, Amina's disruptive behavior seemed to

be contagious. Her classmates started to ask questions in Arabic instead of trying to use English and began handing in assignments late. Their constant chatting in Arabic during lessons made it clear to me that they weren't taking the class seriously, and I started to become extremely concerned that I was losing not only Amina, but the rest of the students in the class.

The situation in my classroom escalated: Amina was no longer speaking any English during class and I found myself interpreting what she was saying into English just to keep the class moving along. Finally, I asked Amina to see me in my office after class. There, Amina shared that she was an "A" student in Arabic, and was concerned that she wasn't doing as well in English. It's rare for a Saudi student to confide in a teacher, as the teacher is often the student's number one source of anxiety. However, Amina did confide in me and shared that she felt anxious when she entered the English classroom and was afraid she might fail her English classes. I tried comforting her, and I attempted to bolster her confidence in herself and her ability, emphasizing that she needed to work a bit harder, concentrate more in class, and practice speaking English with her classmates outside of class.

Although Amina began to use a little English in class, her attendance became spotty—especially when a quiz or presentation was scheduled. Later, I reflected on Amina's behavior and her disclosures in my office. *Why was she becoming anxious when she entered the English language classroom? Why did she compare her performance in English language classes to her performance in Arabic? Was her anxiety causing her to be disruptive in class, or were there other factors at play? And, did her classmates feel anxious, too?*

At the time, I was unaware that disruptive behavior and exaggerated laughing and joking can be manifestations of anxiety. Later, I read Madeline Ehrman's book, *Understanding Second Language Learning Difficulties,* in which she states that disappointment over performance in a language class can lead to anxiety, getting in the way of learning:

> Anxiety is often linked to fear that one will fail in some way: on an assignment, speaking in class, on a test, in the final grade, in competition, maintaining one's position in a community, in interactions with native speakers, or on the job.[1]

Ehrman went on to discuss manifestations of anxiety in the foreign language classroom, explaining that people use defense mechanisms such as being disruptive, joking excessively or laughing, angry outbursts, and impulsive actions and statements to protect their emotions and self-esteem. I'd

---

1. Ehrman, M. E. (1996). *Understanding Second Language Learning Difficulties.* Thousand Oaks, CA: Sage Publications.

observed some of the defense mechanisms she described, and was intrigued by the motivations behind them. According to Ehrman, defense mechanisms are essential for softening failures, protecting oneself from overwhelming anxiety, and maintaining a sense of personal worth—all of which had come into play in my classroom. Given the importance of avoiding failure and saving face (or looking good) in Saudi Arabian culture, some of these strategies might even be more prevalent in Saudi Arabia than in the West.

Later research shed light on other manifestations of foreign language anxiety (FLA), including avoidance behaviors such as showing up to class unprepared, rarely speaking or volunteering to participate, and cutting class. FLA can also have physical symptoms, including fidgeting, stuttering, the jitters, headaches, and tight muscles.[1]

Although I had extensive classroom experience—both as a student and later as a teacher—I'd never considered that students' disruptive behaviors might be defense mechanisms against anxiety. In fact, I found my students' actions somewhat shocking, especially in Saudi Arabia, where learning is greatly valued and teachers are highly regarded. The students were not paying attention, studying, or showing respect to their teacher. However, as I pondered these behaviors in light of the

---

1. Oxford, R. L. (2005). Anxiety and the language learner: New insights. In J. Arnold (Ed.), *Affect in Language Learning* (p. 58). Cambridge University Press.

research I'd discovered, I saw that my students' actions may have been signs of FLA.

My experience with Amina and students like her piqued my interest in FLA, particularly how understanding what was happening in my classes could help me become a better teacher. As an EFL lecturer at an English medium university in Saudi Arabia, I was able to get to know my students and observe their frustrations as they tried to learn English. I also witnessed their struggles to transition from the Saudi Arabian high school system (in which they attended English lessons three or four times per week) to a language program that taught reading and writing, listening and speaking, and grammar—all in English. However, my observations and investigations didn't lead me to any information or resources that could help me improve my students' learning experiences.

So, I decided to further investigate EFL students' struggles and experiences, focusing on the female student population in Saudi Arabia. This marked the beginning of my academic journey toward understanding FLA.

What is Foreign Language Anxiety, or FLA?

Researchers have been examining the anxiety associated with learning a foreign language since the 1960s. In 1986, Elaine K. Horwitz and her colleagues determined that FLA is unique and distinct from other forms of anxiety. FLA is a type of situation-specific anxiety that arises from learning a foreign language. It can be provoked by many specific situations that arise while learning a new language, such as not knowing the meaning of a word or speaking a non-native language in front of peers.

I like to define FLA in a more comprehensive way: Foreign language anxiety is distinct from general anxiety; it's a type of situation anxiety experienced by language learners that arises specifically from learning a second or foreign language. The feelings and behavior associated with FLA can have a positive impact on the language-learning process by motivating the learner; or, they can negatively affect the learner, preventing them from being successful in learning a new language.[2,3]

To learn more about FLA, Horwitz, Horwitz, and Cope created the Foreign Language Classroom Anxiety Scale (FLCAS),

---

2.   Al-Saraj, T. M. (2011). *Exploring foreign language anxiety in Saudi Arabia: A study of female English as foreign language college students*. (Unpublished doctoral dissertation). Institute of Education, University of London.

3.   Al-Saraj, T. M. (2013). Foreign language anxiety in female Arab learners of English in Saudi Arabia: case studies. *Innovation in Language Learning and Teaching,* 1-22. doi: 10.1080/17501229.2013.837911

a questionnaire designed to assess students' issues with learning a foreign language.[4] Since then, this questionnaire, the first tool of its kind, has been used by most researchers delving into FLA, at least those exploring it quantitatively. However, I have found that this questionnaire, developed working with students learning Spanish as a foreign language at the University of Texas, doesn't take into account the varying backgrounds, situations, and experiences of students who might take it. (More on the potential importance of these factors in a few moments.)

In addition to the fact that *most* research has used the FLCAS, only a small number of studies have examined FLA in regions such as Asia and the Middle East; so, relatively little is known about FLA outside of the West. Although researchers have identified some things that provoke FLA (e.g., speaking in the new language), they don't know the underlying cause of FLA. Researchers have also yet to determine exactly how FLA hinders language learning, but it seems apparent that high anxiety and poor performance in the language classroom are related. It also seems that this connection works both ways: Anxiety can lead to difficulty in learning a language, and difficulty in learning a language can bring about anxiety. In addition, the majority of studies have been conducted in the West, with very little attention given to students in Arabic-

---

4. Horwitz, E. K., Horwitz, M. B., & Cope, J. (1986). Foreign language classroom anxiety. *The Modern Language Journal, 70* (2), 125-132.

speaking countries like Saudi Arabia. Given the importance of saving face and not making mistakes in Saudi Arabia, it seems FLA could be incredibly common there! Differences in culture, classroom expectations, and so on must be considered.

In addition to a simple lack of research, I believe that researchers have struggled to fully unravel the complexities of FLA in part because of the tools they have used. Much of the FLA research that's been conducted so far has focused on quantitative data—numbers—rather than on individuals' (qualitative) experiences. The human experience is at the heart of FLA: Foreign language anxiety impacts *people*. Understanding the emotions and motives at play is crucial to gaining a deeper understanding of how anxiety affects foreign language learning, and because of that, I was determined to design a study to explore and better comprehend—qualitatively—students' experiences when learning a foreign language.

My Research

I opted to study FLA in my home country, not only because of my knowledge of Saudi Arabia and my personal connections, but also because studying English is becoming increasingly common there. A unique combination of factors—including the growing importance of learning English, recent changes in the educational system, and the Saudi Arabian culture—created an intriguing environment for studying FLA. I worked with a private, English medium university in Jeddah, Saudi Arabia. Given the segregation of men and women in the Saudi educational system, and given that I am a woman, I worked with a women's university so that I would have access to and be able to talk with the students.

While the Saudi Arabian context is fascinating, it also poses a challenge for anyone who isn't intimately and personally familiar with the culture and educational system; it could be difficult for many researchers to conduct a thorough and culturally sensitive study. As a Saudi Arabian woman who's studied in the United States, Saudi Arabia, and the United Kingdom, and who's taught in Saudi Arabia, I understood this context in a way that few researchers—*especially* Western-educated researchers—would.

A New Questionnaire

Although the FLCAS has been used since the 1980s, it was designed for use in the West—not in the Middle East, where the culture and learning styles differ greatly from those of Western environments. It hasn't been widely employed all over the world in research, and I questioned whether it was appropriate for use in Middle Eastern cultures. *Did the FLCAS address the issues that provoke FLA in Saudi Arabian students? If so, would this existing survey, translated into Arabic, be an effective means of gaining understanding of these students?*

Ultimately, the answer was no. So, I set out to develop a new questionnaire.

I devised a questionnaire appropriate for the Saudi educational and social culture: the Arabic Foreign Language Anxiety Questionnaire (AFLAQ; the full questionnaire can be found in the appendix at the end of this book). This survey would allow me to measure the level of anxiety each student was feeling and identify those students experiencing high levels.

Learning by Listening to Students

When researchers or psychologists examine "case studies," we look at real people in real-life situations, which lets us see what happens out in the world instead of in the laboratory (where situations can be contrived and controlled). Based on their responses to my questionnaire about anxiety, the AFLAQ, I chose 10 students who were attending the English medium university and who reported moderate to high levels of anxiety, and I asked them if I could follow them through an entire semester at the university. I chose five students who were relatively new to the university and had low English skills (in Level 1 of 4 in the program), and five students who were more advanced (in Level 3 of 4). Typical of the students in this program, they were all 18- or 19-year-old Muslim women. Eight of the 10 were from Saudi Arabia, and the others were from nearby Arab countries. This small group would provide me with a window into the nature of FLA in my home country— and how both teachers and students can minimize its negative impact on language learning.

Questionnaires can provide some insight, but I wanted to know what was really going on in students' minds. *What factors do students think are hindering their learning and achievement in the classroom? What factors are taking away from their EFL experience? What would they suggest to improve their experience?*

To help me better understand students' actions, reactions, and emotions in class, I talked with the students individually and in small groups. Most had never been in a situation like that, and at first, they were very uncomfortable being asked to talk openly about their experiences. However, I was surprised by how quickly they adapted and began to speak openly and frankly.

Chapter Five **5**

Uncharted Territory:
Unfamiliar Language,
Unfamiliar Learning

The rest of the English as a Second Language class was engaged in a listening and speaking exercise, but Maha, one of the students in my case studies, didn't say a word. She seemed inattentive to the lesson, but was clearly concentrating on something. Worry was painted across her face.

Earlier that day, Maha's teacher had shared with me that Maha's English skills were very weak, and that each time a quiz was scheduled, Maha would ask to be excused from class or would be absent altogether. Although her teacher had asked her to drop the class and take a semester of non-credit English before returning, Maha had refused, saying she wanted to remain in the same class as her friends.

Despite Maha's claim that she wanted to remain in class with her friends, it wasn't long before she stopped attending class, just a month into the semester. When I called her and suggested that she come to my office so that we could talk, she declined, insisting that she couldn't even set foot on the university grounds. As a Saudi woman, she had a driver take her to the university, but as her car would near the university, her heart would begin pounding so hard in her chest that she felt as though her heart might burst. She recognized that she was panicking, and she described it that way. But, unable to get past her feelings, she would not enter the university and instead had her driver turn around and take her home. Maha also insisted that she wanted to continue in the English program, but simply couldn't.

One of Maha's friends explained to me that Maha believed her negative experiences were due to having a "bad eye," a sort of jinx, which she suspected had befallen her because others were envious that she was attending a relatively prestigious, private, English medium university. However, her description of the reaction she had each time she neared the campus could have come from a textbook on anxiety.

I never saw her again.

A Two-Way Street: Anxiety and Achievement

FLA isn't benign. It's not just a feeling. This anxiety can hinder learning, both by negatively impacting performance in the classroom and by preventing students from continuing their studies. Anxiety isn't always negative, however. We generally need at least a small dose to push us through a challenge. However, when anxiety becomes too great, it interferes with learning. The key is to lower anxiety so that there's enough to provide motivation, but not so much that it becomes overwhelming. The impact of anxiety on foreign language learning isn't mere conjecture, and in recent decades researchers have gathered evidence of the tangible ways that FLA can negatively affect achievement in the classroom. Horwitz and her colleagues found that FLA had a significant negative impact on students' grades in a foreign language course. Students who demonstrated high levels of FLA not only expected lower grades than their less anxious classmates expected, they actually received lower grades than their counterparts. This relationship is also true in reverse: Students who don't perform as well in class tend to experience higher levels of anxiety.[1] This can create a vicious cycle in which anxiety and lack of achievement feed into one another and snowball into a larger problem.

The connection between anxiety and poor grades may be due in part to the fact that students who are anxious may be hesitant to participate in class. Students who reported high levels of anxiety reported feeling extremely self-conscious when they were asked to speak the language they were trying to learn in front of others.[2] This self-consciousness may prevent them from doing the very thing they need to do to improve: practice. (More on this in Chapter Six.)

Poor grades—both fear of them and actually receiving

1. Batumlu, Z. D., & Erden, M. (2007). The relationship between foreign language anxiety and English achievement of Yildiz Technical University, School of Foreign Languages preparatory students. *Journal of Theory and Practice in Education*, 3(1), 24-38.
2.   Horwitz, E. K., Horwitz, M. B., & Cope, J. (1986). Foreign language classroom anxiety. *The Modern Language Journal, 70*(2), 125-132.

them—are common causes of anxiety even in familiar learning environments. When this anxiety is coupled with the struggles of navigating unfamiliar learning methods, it can become overwhelming. This can be especially true for those who performed well in the high school classroom and are unaccustomed to receiving bad grades.

This was true of Maha. She shared with me that she had received good grades in high school, but wasn't earning high grades in the university. She didn't feel prepared for the EFL program and, as her performance in class suggested, she wasn't prepared for the unfamiliar teaching methods. Based on her performance in high school, Maha had seen herself as a good student and expected to earn good grades in university. For her and many like her who had been accustomed to success in the rote learning environment, earning an undesirable grade in a university course adds yet another level of unfamiliarity, and can compound anxiety.

While a small amount of anxiety can serve to motivate a student to improve his or her performance, a high level of anxiety often has the opposite effect. Maha's anxiety was so severe that she repeatedly experienced acute physical symptoms and couldn't even walk into the classroom.

So, what causes anxiety that leads to lower grades or students dropping out of a program? The answer isn't the same for everyone, but a number of factors are common causes. The students in my study often cited teaching methods, interaction with teachers, grades, speaking in class, and giving in-class presentations when talking about their struggles to learn English.

In the rest of this chapter, I'll explain how the method of education and teaching styles can contribute to FLA. Then, in Chapter Six, I'll focus on how many of the other commonly cited sources of anxiety relate to the desire to save face and the difficulty of communicating in an unfamiliar language.

Ill-Prepared: From Rote Learning to Interactive Education

Regulations in Saudi Arabia mandate that English is taught beginning in year four, when students are nine or 10 years old. Ultimately, few students become fluent enough to use English on the job, despite the fact that they spend an average of four hours a week in English study for at least nine years. In fact, at the end of secondary school, the majority of students are only able to speak in memorized sentences—they can't form new, correct English sentences of their own.[3]

---

3. Al-Ghamdi, A. (2005). Who is to blame in English fluency: Curriculum or method? *Okaz Newspaper*, Jeddah, 14289:25.

Why can't these students create original sentences in English after nearly a decade of studying the language? The grammar-translation method of teaching English, the prominent method in Saudi Arabia, is a huge contributing factor. In classes that use this method, students memorize grammatical rules and then apply those rules by translating sentences from one language to another, typically verbally (out loud). Memorization is a cornerstone of this method. In the end, students can restate what they've been taught, but they can't apply it. Students do drill-type exercises, but little attention is given to pronunciation—a key component of being able to clearly communicate.[4,5] I am not in any way blaming only the grammar-translation method for this, but I believe it is one major contributor, especially in a time of great technological advancement.

Exams are the only measure of a student's progress. As a result, students often focus their efforts on memorizing the information that will be on the exam—not on grasping the language itself. Maha, who struggled so much with just attending the college, aptly described how she was taught in high school. She was given three sheets of paper to study before exams and quizzes, and the exam questions would come

4. Brown, H. D. (2007). *Principles of language learning and teaching* (5th ed.). White Plains, NY: Pearson Education, Inc.
5. Richard-Amato, P. A. (2010). *Making it Happen from Interactive to Participatory Language Teaching: Evolving Theory and Practice* (4th ed.). White Plains, NY: Pearson Education, Inc.

from those mere three sheets. She was not expected to seek out information or question anything: From seventh grade through 12th grade, all she did was memorize the contents of those three sheets. It was not necessary to understand anything, one weakness of this rote learning method. She entered the university not grasping English, having learned only to memorize and not to question or understand.

As a result of this memorization-heavy method, students entering English medium universities enter as passive learners. They come from years in classrooms in which teachers dominate and students aren't required to do much more than sit and soak up information. Most students coming out of high school and entering English as a Foreign Language (EFL) programs at English medium universities or colleges have never learned to do more than mimic the words and phrases they've been taught. While being able to repeat a sentence can be helpful in a specific situation, accurate, meaningful communication requires an understanding of how sentences are created—not mere regurgitation. But, when they begin their studies at English medium universities, students are expected to interact, apply their knowledge, and take initiative. They are overwhelmed by these new tasks and demands, and underprepared for the Western style of education.

Not surprisingly, many of these ill-prepared English students fear failure. In fact, when students in Level 1 took the AFLAQ, they agreed with the statement, "I fear failing my foreign language class" more than any other statement. Fear of failure was also a big concern for students in Level 3, ranking third. This fear wasn't irrational. Three of the students participating in my study—nearly a third of participants—failed the semester. While it's impossible to say just how much anxiety played a role in their final grades, it's entirely possible that their fear of failure served as a self-fulfilling prophecy: By dreading failure, they made failure more likely.

A New Method of Learning

Much of the Saudi English language students' experiences in the classroom can be summed up in a word: unfamiliar. In contrast to the Saudi Arabian public educational system, English medium universities in the country tend to use Western, interactive means of instruction. As a result, the young women who participated in my study were tackling a new means of learning in addition to a new language. Not only were these students expected to take part in unfamiliar activities in class, their performance in these activities was *evaluated* and played a role in their final grades. This, too, was uncharted territory.

Tackling new methods of learning and evaluation can be challenging at best, and the cause of debilitating language anxiety at worst. For example, students entering these English language programs at English medium universities often have little (if any) experience with speaking in class or giving presentations—in any subject, much less in a foreign language. The research I'd conducted to create the AFLAQ provided me with insights into just how much this inexperience contributes to FLA. I'd asked students to give examples of times they feel anxious or nervous in the English language classroom, encouraging them to think of as many examples as they could. Of the 48 students who responded, 20 of them (over 40 percent!) mentioned giving a presentation in front of the class. In fact, students mentioned giving a presentation more than any other anxiety-causing situation, citing it at least twice as often as any other scenario. This took me by surprise. Until that point, when I would hear students say that they didn't want to give a presentation, I would assume it was because they didn't know how—I never realized that presentations caused so much anxiety for so many Saudi students. It was then that it occurred to me that I never gave presentations in high school—and neither had they. Giving a presentation was an unfamiliar, nerve-wracking experience for them, even without the added anxiety of trying to speak in a foreign language.

Anxiety during presentations also came up frequently when I was talking with the students in my case studies. One of these students, Noura, said that in-class presentations were an anxiety-ridden experience because she was supposed to understand what she was saying, not memorize or read it. In addition, students are suddenly expected to use other presentation skills, such as making eye contact, that they had never learned or practiced in their native language, much less in English. As Noura explained, the situation felt out of her control, and she easily lost her place in her presentation, especially if she was interrupted.

Noura, like many of her classmates, was discovering that communicating in a foreign language is a far cry from simply reciting sentences. Students like her often have little experience in speaking in English without a script, but when they enter college- or university-level programs with Western teaching methods that are unfamiliar to them, they're suddenly expected not only to speak in sentences they've formed themselves, but to do so in front of others, making giving presentations a doubly anxiety-provoking experience.

One of Noura's classmates, Youssra, said she was extremely anxious to present in front of other students. She was afraid that the presentations that came before hers would be better than hers, and that the teacher would criticize her. She actually preferred to not do the presentation (and have points deducted from her grade) than to do the presentation and receive a bad grade.

Presentations are far from the only unfamiliar situations that provoke anxiety in English classrooms in Saudi Arabia. Any exercise that requires speaking can become a dreaded activity. Several studies have shown that speaking in a foreign language tends to be more anxiety-provoking than other tasks related to language learning.[6,7,8] When students are accustomed to merely reciting as opposed to speaking in an effort to communicate their own ideas, this anxiety is magnified.

Sabah, also in Noura's class, summed it all up, saying that she and her classmates were anxious simply because they were not used to speaking English.

6. Daly, J. A. (1991). Understanding communication apprehension: An introduction for language educators. In E. K. Horwitz & D. J. Young (Eds.), *Language Anxiety: From Theory and Research to Classroom Implications* (pp. 3-13). Englewood Cliffs, NJ: Prentice Hall.
7. Price, M. L. (1991). The subjective experience of foreign language anxiety: Interviews with highly anxious students. In E. K. Horwitz & D. J. Young (Eds.), *Language Anxiety: From Theory and Research to Classroom Implications.* Upper Saddle River, NJ: Prentice Hall.
8. Young, D.J. (1999). Affect in Foreign Language and Second Language Learning. Boston, MA: McGraw Hill

Chapter Six 6

Saving Face and Redefining Self

Language learning doesn't happen in a vacuum. It's a social activity that involves using new words that follow new rules, making it next to impossible to learn a language without making a host of blunders—and making them in front of others. And, it's deeply influenced by culture.

Like a pair of tinted glasses, culture colors the way a person views the world, and language is an inextricable part of culture. Danish scholar Karen Risager proposed that, "Human culture always includes language, and human language cannot be conceived without culture." In other words, you can't separate language and culture, and can't look at one without considering the other. From this perspective, language is actually culture in linguistic form.[1]

Cultures vary greatly, and as a result, students experience FLA differently from culture to culture—students in Saudi Arabia don't experience FLA in the same way that students in the United States do. The situations that prompt anxiety and the behaviors that express it vary depending on the culture. For example, in some cultures (like traditional Saudi culture), remaining quiet in class is a sign of respect for the teacher; however, in other cultures (such as the English medium university) speaking in class is expected behavior. In addition, individuals interpret all of their experiences, including their

1. Risager, K. (2006). *Language and Culture: Global Flows and Local Complexity*. Clevedon, UK: Multilingual Matters, 4.

anxiety, through the lens of their culture—for example, Maha suspected she'd been jinxed.

Both the culture of the person learning a language and the culture associated with the language the student is learning play a role in FLA, because the way in which language is used is tied closely to culture.[2] That's why it's so important to carefully consider the cultural context when studying FLA. It's also why I created a survey—that takes into account the teaching styles used in the Saudi culture—that specifically addresses the unique ways in which FLA is expressed in this culture.

New Language, New Identity?

So, if language and culture are so closely connected, does that mean that students adopt a new identity when they learn a new language? In many ways, yes, especially when the culture of the new language is very different from a student's native culture (as was the case in the English language program where I conducted my research). It's also particularly true when the student wants to interact with others in the new language.

Gaining a new language often means gaining a new identity based in a new culture. Professor and scholar Dr. Bonny

---

2.   Kramsch, C. (2001). *Language and Culture.* Oxford, UK: Oxford University Press.

Norton explains identity as "how a person understands his or her relationship with the world, how that relationship is constructed across time and space and how the person understands possibilities for the future."[3] Language is intimately involved in shaping identity, because it's through language that individuals interact with others and learn cultural norms.

Learning a new language involves not only coming to understand new words and grammar, but also new ways of doing things. Language learners pick up on what's acceptable and what's not in the culture of the new language. In this sense, a new language conditions those who learn it to operate in a specific way when they speak it, and the more they progress in their language ability, the more they learn how to operate in that language's culture.

The more a language student learns, the more they begin to construct a second identity that corresponds to the new language, and begin to switch back and forth between cultures depending upon what language they're speaking. For example, I act very differently when speaking English in the United States than I would in Saudi Arabia or even in the United Kingdom, because I've learned what's considered normal in American culture. In ways, I temporarily change my identity in order to blend in when I'm in the United States.

---

3.   Norton, Bonny. (2000). *Identity and Language Learning: Gender, Ethnicity and Cultural Change.* London, UK: Pearson Education Limited, 5.

I saw signs of similar changes in the students in my case studies. While I didn't have the opportunity to observe students as they progressed throughout the English language program, I saw evidence of the ways they had adapted to the Western culture of the university. The most obvious difference between the students in Level 1 and the students in Level 3 was how they dressed. The Level 1 students, who were usually fresh out of high school, stood out due to their conservative attire: Each of them dressed in loose, plain clothing, usually wearing long skirts. And, most of them opted to wear an abaya even inside the university, even though no men were present and most of the other students wore more Western-style clothing while on campus. The students in Level 1 may have chosen to dress as they did because they were shy, reserved, or simply conservative; or, they may have simply been dressing as they were accustomed to dressing—the Western influence of the university was still new to them.

In contrast, most of the students in Level 3 appeared to be attempting to blend in with the student body. They generally sported Western clothes and hairstyles—and did so with confidence. As students who'd already completed at least one semester of the EFL program at the university, they seemed decidedly more confident than students in Level 1, and tended to mix freely with the mainstream university students.

The differences between the two groups went beyond

appearances. The Level 1 students seemed to respect and perhaps even revere their teachers, and rarely questioned them, a reflection of the traditional Saudi view of teachers. Although they may have hesitated to challenge their teachers due to the language barrier, it is my opinion that they refrained from questioning because they were still accustomed to and acting in accordance with the Saudi Arabian educational system.

By the time students reached Level 3, they seemed to have acclimated to the Western learning environment within the classroom and within the English medium university. Due to their experience, they were more familiar with the methods and teaching style used at the university, and more comfortable in the EFL program. Unlike the generally passive learners in Level 1, the students I observed in Level 3 were much more assertive and actively participated in class. They gave suggestions to the teacher and even regularly bargained with her in efforts to get her to reschedule deadlines or give them more time to prepare for presentations. These bold actions would have been unthinkable to the students in Level 1.

Despite the ways in which most of the Level 3 students seemed to have adapted to the Western learning environment, all of the students in my study still experienced their anxiety through the lens of a Saudi context. And, in Saudi culture, it all ties back to saving face.

Saving Face

The concept of saving face is woven into Saudi culture, and it's very closely linked to self-worth. Self-respect is held in the highest regard and is to be maintained at all times; when a person "loses face," that person loses self-respect. Loss of face is more than temporary embarrassment: It entails shame as well as losing respect. Although the concept of "saving face" is familiar to most people in the West, few understand the depth and severity with which it's experienced in Saudi and Arab culture. There's no real Western equivalent to this degree of saving face, and it can be difficult to understand for those who haven't lived in a culture that values face to fully understand its impact. However, for Saudis, face is *always* a consideration, and it plays a big role in FLA.

Like children learning their mother tongue for the first time, students tackling a foreign language often learn by trial and error as they try new vocabulary and apply unfamiliar rules of grammar. They make a lot of mistakes, and it's through those mistakes that they learn. However, in Saudi culture, mistakes aren't just brushed off or taken lightly—because a mistake causes a person to lose face. As a result, many English language students hesitate to speak in class because a blunder is more than just a simple misstep, and may lead to far more than momentary embarrassment. Speaking in class is seen as a risky endeavor. If a student answers a question incorrectly, mispronounces a word, or even speaks less than fluently, fellow classmates—or, even worse, the teacher—might laugh at or even think less of him or her. Often, students simply avoid this risk altogether. In Maha's case, dropping the course entirely was preferable to making a mistake in class and feeling foolish in front of everyone.

In Western culture, if you make a mistake, you just try again and it's perfectly acceptable to keep trying until you succeed. Sure, there might be some embarrassment along the way, but making mistakes and trying again are generally viewed as part of the learning process. In Saudi culture, there's pressure to get it right the first time, because if you don't, no one will take you seriously. If you try again, it's assumed that you'll just fail as you did before, and then you'll constantly be the laughing stock of the town. Of course this is not always true with everyone in the culture, but it is the overwhelmingly prevalent mindset.

Since I spent much of my childhood in the West, I tend to laugh at my mistakes, pick myself up, and try again, something that's uncommon in the Saudi culture. To the vast majority of my students, laughing off a mistake was unthinkable. Students don't want to make mistakes because they don't want others to think they're stupid. If someone cracks a joke or laughs at the students' expense, it's as if their world implodes.

Remember Amina, the student in my English class who first prompted me to study FLA? She was afraid that if she didn't say something right, the other students would laugh at her, even though I repeatedly assured the class that, "We laugh together, not at one another." I didn't make the connection at the time, but I now see that she was desperately trying to save face.

In light of saving face, any opportunity to make a mistake— essentially any activity that requires students to speak— becomes an open invitation for anxiety. Being put on the spot can be especially anxiety-provoking for many students because it requires them to think on the spot, making mistakes more likely. In fact, on the AFLAQ, the statement, "I feel anxious when the teacher asks me a question that I have not prepared for," was ranked in the top five causes of FLA by students in both Level 1 and Level 3.

In turn, anxiety over the possibility of looking foolish in front of others hinders students' ability to speak as well as they'd be able to if no one were listening and they were unconcerned with how they'd look. I felt this keenly in my efforts to learn Turkish. Not only did I try to figure out what question I'd be asked ahead of time while sitting in class, I'd practice paragraphs in Turkish at home or in the car so I'd be prepared when the teacher called on me in class and asked me to talk about myself.

One day as I was sitting in my car on the way to my Turkish class in London, I turned off the radio and started talking to myself in Turkish. As I sat there at the intersection of Wigmore and Regent Streets, I practiced introducing myself, describing how my day was going, and describing my plans for the weekend—all things I knew I'd have to do in class. My conversation with myself seemed quite fluent and I was impressed with myself for making up several sentences of my own in Turkish. Minutes later, I managed to park my car on the overcrowded streets of London—a miracle. I walked to class with a confident spring in my step. I was playing a scenario in my head and it went like this: *When I speak in class today, I'm going to nail it. My teacher will be so impressed!* I felt confident while entering the classroom and during class until it was my turn to speak: I couldn't form a single sentence without stumbling. I was shocked. I honestly didn't know what had happened and I felt like it wasn't really me talking. Then, on top of it all, I blurted out in front of the class, "I practiced saying this at home and in the car, and it went really well—nothing like what I just demonstrated."

Oh my GOD! Did I just say that out loud? I thought to myself. Then to prove me right, I heard the laughs of my teacher and classmates, confirming that yes, I did blurt it out! "Oh, well," I thought to myself. "It's only a language class." I went on to remind myself that I already speak two languages. But, on the way to my car as well as on the drive home, I played what had happened to me in class over and over in my head. *Why was I stumbling? Why wouldn't the words come out right? Why did I forget the words I already knew?* Questions like these spun round and round in my mind.

As I reflected on my experience in my journal that night, I remembered one of my interviews: Zakia, another student in my case studies. I'd noticed that Zakia had a hard time responding when she was called upon in class, and I asked her how she felt when she was asked to answer a question. She responded, "I don't know. I felt that I knew what to say, but I forgot how to read." Even though she'd written her answer ahead of time and had it right in front of her, she'd struggled to get the words out. *Just like me.*

The desire to save face not only causes anxiety that makes it harder to speak in a new language; it can cause students to hesitate to try their language skills in class or even prevent them from speaking at all. For example, many of the students in my study avoided giving live presentations by recording themselves reading the presentation in advance, and then playing the recordings in class. In a group interview, I asked the students why they chose a pre-recorded presentation over a live one. At first, they said it was because the subject matter wasn't suited for a live presentation, but when I pressed them further, several of them admitted that they found it difficult to speak in front of the class. Tamara, one of the students in Level 3, said that she became anxious quickly and easily, and when she became anxious, she forgot what she was trying to say. This tendency to become anxious and lose concentration when speaking in front of the class seemed quite common among my research participants.

Even when the students gave pre-recorded presentations, saving face still came into play. Several students said they felt nervous while their recorded presentations were playing, and Sara explained that this was because of fear of negative evaluation from the other students and the teacher. Would the other students like the presentation? Would they be able to understand her recorded voice? Or, would they think that she sounded dumb or made no sense? Even though she wasn't presenting live, Sara feared being looked down upon by her classmates. However, at the end of the semester, Sara was the only student who opted to give a live presentation. She admitted she was anxious, but it seems that her level of anxiety was low enough that it motivated her to work hard rather than discouraging her and hindering her learning.

Of course, Sara was an exception. Most students struggling with FLA aren't motivated by their anxiety. In fact, in many cases, the students I observed were aware that their anxiety-driven behaviors interfered with their ability to learn, but they seemed unable to stop. For instance, Zakia knew that she needed to interact with her fellow students and participate in class if she wanted to improve her language learning (which would eventually improve her grades), but the semester was well underway before she began to participate.

The fact that Zakia became more accustomed to the Western learning environment over the course of the semester may have played a role in her ability to assume a more active role in her learning. Familiarity with both the culture of the classroom and with the students in it can make a big difference in how much anxiety students feel. In many ways, the desire to save face is compounded by the fact that (as discussed in the previous chapter) many Saudi students are inexperienced in Western teaching methods. As they become more comfortable in a Western learning environment, they may gain confidence to speak—and to risk making the mistakes that lead to learning, and that are inevitable in the learning process.

The Struggle for Self-Expression

Have you ever tried to explain a complex idea to a 4-year-old? Say, gravity? If so, you've likely tasted the challenge of communicating when your language is basic but the concepts you're trying to convey are complicated. Adult language learners face a similar challenge: They're equipped with only a rudimentary understanding of the language they're seeking to learn, but are still thinking at an adult level.

When you're struggling to speak in an unfamiliar language, you might feel as though, no matter how hard you try, you can't communicate who you really are. Conveying what you'd really like to convey—the whole point of speaking in the first place— gets lost in the strenuous task of finding the right words. This mismatch between the level of language ability and the level of thought not only makes it difficult to communicate clearly, but it can also result in frustration and anxiety.

For most adults, being able to clearly convey ideas is a given; learning a new language turns that given on its head. Rather than feeling competent and confident in their ability to communicate—what they've long known as "normal"— language learners may feel self-conscious or fearful, or even experience a sense of panic. This self-consciousness and fear may stem from that underlying sense of inauthenticity that language learners often feel when they try to communicate in a language in which they're not yet fluent.[4] Communication in a new language lacks the nuance of communication in a student's native language, and students may feel as if they're never able to say what they truly mean: They can only skirt around it. Despite their best efforts, they don't feel at home in their new language, and attempting to communicate in it is not only strenuous, but also puts them at risk of losing face.

---

4.   Horwitz, E. K., Horwitz, M. B., & Cope, J. (1986). Foreign language classroom anxiety. *The Modern Language Journal, 70*(2), 125-132.

Challenging Self-Views

In addition to the frustration and anxiety that result when language learners can't convey their thoughts, students of a foreign language often face a crisis of identity. Second language specialist Valerie A. Pellegrino Aveni wrote, "The process of language study is like no other. To learn another language is to redefine yourself publicly, socially, and personally. No other topic of education so deeply affects the individual's own self-presentation in society."[5]

As adults try to communicate in an unfamiliar language, their views of themselves as intelligent and skillful communicators are challenged.[6] Individuals who usually see themselves as good students find themselves struggling to get the grades they're accustomed to earning. Those who see themselves as socially competent may feel unsure of how they're being perceived by others when they're trying to communicate in their new language. Language learners are forced to present themselves as rudimentary-level communicators, an identity that's at odds with the views they've long held about themselves. This is unsettling to say the least, and (not surprisingly) it's yet another factor that leads to anxiety.

---

5.   Aveni, V. A. P. (2005). *Study Abroad and Second Language Use: Constructing the Self*. Cambridge, UK: Cambridge University Press, 7.
6.   Horwitz, E. K., Horwitz, M. B., & Cope, J. (1986). Foreign language classroom anxiety. *The Modern Language Journal, 70*(2), 125-132.

Chapter Seven **7**

How Teachers Can Reduce FLA in Their Classrooms

When I began my research on FLA, I focused on language learners, believing that understanding them would be key to understanding FLA. However, I found the role of teachers to be central in FLA. Many teachers believe that a student's personality is a key factor in whether that student will be successful in learning a new language.[1] I believe that any student can learn to speak a new language. Yes, an extrovert who is highly confident might be more prone to practicing speaking; and, indeed, shy learners tend to be the most anxious.[2] However, an anxious student can learn with adequate support.

One of my goals in writing this book is to increase teachers' awareness of FLA and the negative impact it has on learning. FLA is still a relatively new field and many educators aren't familiar with its symptoms—but it's critical that they become familiar!

In 2012, I was the plenary speaker for a conference organized by the English department of the Saudi Ministry of Education in Jeddah. There were at least 100 English language teachers at my talk. I'd longed for an opportunity like this: Where else would I get a better chance to address English language teachers in Saudi Arabia and explain to them what language anxiety is, what its symptoms are, and how it can affect students? As I shared about FLA, these teachers' jaws dropped. I could see their

1. Ellis, R. (2003). *Task-Based Learning and Teaching.* Oxford: Oxford University Press.
2. Oxford, R. (1989). *The Role of Styles and Strategies in Second Language Learning.* ERIC Digest., ERIC Clearinghouse.

eyes opening, and some just kept nodding their heads as they connected what I was saying to what they were experiencing in their language classrooms. Most of them were floored to learn that their students were experiencing anxiety—much less to discover that they, as teachers, were playing a role in that anxiety. Once they absorbed the initial shock, they wanted to know, "How can we reduce students' anxiety?"

At that conference, I was honored to be able to share a number of strategies that can enable language teachers to reduce FLA in their classrooms, and I'll share many of these strategies in this chapter. It's my goal to empower language teachers to not only recognize FLA in their students, but to help their students overcome their anxiety. The first step is understanding the role the teachers plays in contributing to or easing students' anxiety.

From the Students' Perspective: The Role of the Teacher

When I speak about FLA, teachers often come up to me and tell me that they're surprised that they're causing anxiety in their classrooms. The idea that teachers cause anxiety isn't news to students, however: The students in my study often said that the teacher was largely responsible for their anxiety. One of them, Hind, explained that "the teacher plays a leading role in making the students feel anxious or not anxious," stating that the interactions between teachers and students directly affect students' levels of anxiety.

Farida, in Level 3, summed up the opinion of many students: "The teacher is the main factor… she [the teacher] makes you like or hate the subject … Even when the subject is difficult and we can't stand it, a teacher has the ability to make the girls like it." She claimed that in the previous semester, she had participated in class because her teacher had encouraged and supported her; but, in the current semester, she started to hate her English class because the teacher paid far more attention to the more outgoing students in class, and because the teacher spoke "in a monotone."

Before we dig into the ways in which the teacher plays a role in FLA, it's important to note that, in some cases, students may see their teachers as responsible for factors that are out of teachers' control. Many language learners—particularly those in the early stages of learning—are going through major life changes. Not only are they acclimating to changes in teaching methods and new expectations, but they are adjusting to college life in general. These changes can be stressful, and in the midst of this stress, students may consider the teacher as the primary source (or even the sole source) of their anxiety, when in reality, a number of other factors are at play. Since the teacher is the one who is requiring students to participate in unfamiliar tasks or take on new responsibilities, some students may see the teacher as the only cause of the anxiety they feel. For example, Farida shared, "If the teacher isn't good, for example, if her teaching is different from what I am used to, I feel I will fail in the subject." Farida, like many language learners, equated an unfamiliar teaching style with poor teaching. She went on to explain that she thought that the teacher was to blame for her struggle to write an essay and that her teacher's style prevented her from participating in class.

That said, the teacher does play a huge role. Nearly all language students want to impress the teacher, myself included— remember how hard I practiced my answers to my Turkish teacher's questions? This makes the teacher's support—or lack thereof—a major factor in how much anxiety students feel in the foreign language classroom. Many of the students in my study said that they'd sought feedback, correction, and support from the teacher, but hadn't received it. A lack of support can put a damper on motivation, and I saw a prime example of this in Tamara. She reminded me of myself in many ways: When I interviewed her she spoke energetically and struck me as strong, confident, and independent. Although Tamara's Turkish father believed that women don't need a high level of education and was opposed to her even going to university, Tamara convinced him to permit her to study at the English medium university by arguing that she could study a topic that would not put her in direct contact with men. She even obtained a scholarship.

Obviously determined, Tamara described herself as an excellent student, and her motivation to succeed in university and do something with her life was evident in her efforts to speak in class. However, she shared with me that when she asked her teacher what she could do to earn a higher grade in the listening and speaking class, the teacher laughed as if Tamara were joking. Embarrassed, Tamara didn't seek help from her teacher again. If I put myself in Tamara's shoes, I think I would be completely embarrassed, too. Who would want to repeat that question again, in front of the entire class, in hope of getting through to the teacher? I wouldn't—that's for sure!

Tamara was insightful and reflective when considering how not receiving positive feedback impacted her. She said that when she was giving a presentation in class, even a little praise would improve her spirit, help her relax, and reassure her that the teacher saw how hard she was working. Lack of support from the teacher seemed to sap Tamara's motivation, and her resolve faded as the semester wore on. She began procrastinating on assignments and avoiding work altogether. She ultimately earned a final grade of a C for the semester—hardly characteristic of a self-professed "excellent student."

Although Tamara wanted feedback, many students find it difficult to receive feedback—even when it's positive. Despite their concerns about not receiving constructive feedback, many students are pulled both ways when it comes to being corrected by the teacher: While they recognize that receiving guidance from the teacher would help them learn, being corrected can be a very upsetting experience. Sara expressed this tension, calling being corrected by her teacher "the end of the world," but also complaining that her teacher didn't offer constructive feedback. She wanted guidance and constructive criticism, though she knew it would be hard to hear. How else would she learn?

Several students also shared that some teachers seem to focus on the students who are more vocal in class, giving less attention and praise to students who aren't talkative. Tamara said that the teachers simply prefer the students who show off in class. I find it very interesting that Tamara uses the term "show off." In her eyes, you are showing off if you speak in class. It also provides a hint about what students are accustomed to doing in their classrooms: It's common to stay quiet even if you know the answers. Here's a good example of how learning style and teaching methods have a large impact on the language learner and how, in order to succeed in learning a new language, students must let go of their past learning styles and break out of their shells. This concept applies not only to students, but to teachers as well: Don't resist experimenting with new teaching styles and new ways of learning.

I asked the students how they felt when the teacher concentrated on the more outgoing students and heard a common theme throughout their answers: They developed negative feelings about English class when they felt they were ignored and the other students were favored. They stopped wanting to come to class.

The students in my study repeatedly told me how favoritism, lack of support, and lack of positive feedback took a toll on them in the classroom. However, they also shared that the flipside could be true as well: Receiving support, attention, and constructive criticism would help them learn.

So, how can teachers give students the kind of support that helps them overcome anxiety? I believe a coaching approach is a big part of the answer.

The Teacher as a Coach

Coaching has become a buzzword in many circles, but it has yet to fully penetrate academia. Shortly before I began studying Turkish, I was introduced to coaching via a free seminar, and I was hooked immediately. I loved that, in coaching, no one can dictate what you are to do. You are free to choose what you want to do, but the coach (sometimes called a "life coach") will help you get there. I loved the fact that the coach can enable you to focus on the goals you're trying to achieve while holding you accountable to accomplish them. As someone who loves teaching and helping others, I started connecting this method with education in general and then specifically with language learning. I wondered how my students might benefit from coaching. *Why can't the teacher be the coach within the classroom?*

The International Coach Federation (ICF) defines coaching as:

> Partnering with clients in a thought-provoking and creative process that inspires them to maximize their personal and professional potential, which is particularly important in today's uncertain and complex environment. Coaches honor the client as the expert in his or her life and work and believe every client is creative, resourceful and whole. Standing on this foundation, the coach's responsibility is to:
> - *Discover, clarify, and align with what the client wants to achieve*
> - *Encourage client self-discovery*
> - *Elicit client-generated solutions and strategies*
> - *Hold the client responsible and accountable*
>
> This process helps clients dramatically improve their outlook on work and life, while improving their leadership skills and unlocking their potential.[1]

---

1. International Coach Federation: Coaching FAQS. Retrieved from http://coachfederation.org/need/landing.cfm? ItemNumber=978

The bottom line is that coaching is all about asking just the right questions to get individuals to discover their own solutions. So, what if the teacher becomes the coach in the classroom? What if English teachers were to ask their students just the right questions to uncover the students' motivation for studying this new language, for example? I believe if teachers were to adopt more of a coaching approach instead of using the rote method or spoon-feeding their students the information, then students would become autonomous learners—less anxious ones.

After participating in the complimentary coaching seminar, I decided to become a certified coach myself. One of the requirements for becoming a certified coach is that you must experience the coaching process with a senior coach. My coach and I talked on the telephone throughout my yearlong certification process. It just so happened that I had a telephone session with my coach on the same day that I panicked when having to take the Turkish exam at Berkeley. The conversation went something like this:

> Me: *I panicked today when I had to take my Turkish exam. I'd gotten up at 4 o'clock in the morning to study. I thought I knew it all, and then when I looked at the exam, I didn't understand a thing. I didn't finish the test. It was terrible.*
>
> Coach: *So why do you think that happened?*
>
> Me: *I was so anxious over the test. I'm auditing this language*

course, but if it had been a course for credit, I would have failed. I mean, I truly would have flunked.

Coach: *I'm curious... What is your deadline for learning Turkish?*

Me (Surprised): *I don't have one. There is no deadline.*

Coach: *So learning Turkish is something you've chosen to do on your own. For what reason?*

Me: *For research purposes. I'm using myself as a guinea pig so I can see what it's like to be in the shoes of the students I've studied and learn how foreign language anxiety affects me.*

Coach: *What I'm hearing is that learning Turkish is something you've decided to do as part of your research. It's for your own enjoyment and has nothing to do with your job.*

Me: *That's correct.*

Coach: *How long have you been taking Turkish classes?*

Me: *Almost a year now.*

Coach: *So, when is your due date to finish this research?*

Me: *There is no end date. I decide when to stop and write up my research.*

Coach: *What I hear you saying is that you are in control of when to stop this research.*

Me: *Yes.*

Coach: *And what is stopping you from completing it?*

Me: *Nothing ...* (long pause) *I guess because I'm an overachiever, I feel that I have not yet mastered the language; therefore, my research would not be complete if I stop now, when I'm not fluent in the language. I guess this is my own personality affecting my research, which in reality should not be the case. I'm doing this research to see if I, an experienced language anxiety researcher, would experience language anxiety myself and to see what my language students felt like and how I can reduce the effects of anxiety.*

Coach: *So, what I understand from what you have said is that you're putting the pressure on yourself to continue this research.*

Me: *Yes, big time! I wanted to do this research while enjoying the language learning process. But the way I'm going now, I'm not enjoying it at all. I feel guilty if I miss class because of my work and family time. I feel disappointed that I'm not producing as much as I should. I think I'm less fluent than the rest of the class. I guess I'm just overwhelmed.*

Coach: *How can you be less overwhelmed while learning the language?*

Me: (a long pause) … *I know from research that learning a language in an academic setting is more likely to be anxiety-provoking, but learning it in a more friendly way is less anxiety-provoking.*

At that point, the light bulb went on.

Me: *Yes, I've got it! I heard there's a Turkish Cultural Center near Berkeley. I could continue studying Turkish there. I think this would reduce my stress as I'd be less focused on academic achievement.*

As soon as I got off the phone with my coach, I emailed my Turkish teacher to ask if it was okay if I stopped auditing the class, and he had no problem with it. I now take Turkish lessons at the local Turkish Cultural Center on Saturday mornings. This may not seem like a big revelation to you, but it was to me. I was so wrapped up in my own anxiety over the Turkish test, I couldn't see the forest for the trees. I forgot why I was even taking Turkish in the first place—for research and fun! And I certainly wasn't having any fun. During my conversation with my coach, I also realized that studying Turkish had become a stressor to me because it was detracting from my ability to have time with my family, particularly my 10-year-old son who was at Berkeley with me. Finding a solution that allowed me to still study Turkish and also have that time with my son was a huge relief.

Coaching helped me get to the truth of the matter for myself; it helped me examine my motivation for learning Turkish. Similarly, I believe when language teachers begin to ask their students some open-ended questions, they will be given information they can use to design classes and motivate students. Coaching also provides students with an opportunity to see the obstacles they face from a different angle, and to discover alternate solutions that enable them to move forward rather than giving up.

Tapping into Students' Motivations

A coaching approach is an excellent way to tap into students' motivations for learning English. Motivation is a must. If students aren't motivated, they won't be driven to continue learning the language or to overcome language anxiety, if they suffer from it. Why put forth the effort to reach a goal they're not enthused about?

Take Maha, for example. She didn't have that motivation and when she was consumed with anxiety, she simply stopped attending class. In contrast, Hind's high level of motivation served her well. Even though Hind's responses on the AFLAQ indicated that she was more anxious than any of the other Level 1 students in my study, she successfully passed the course. Although she felt out of place and ill-prepared at the beginning of the semester, she pushed herself to catch up with her classmates. Although I didn't have the opportunity to ask Hind directly about her motivation for studying English, I learned she was planning to travel to Canada in the coming summer so that she could stay with her cousin and practice her English. Knowing that she'd be traveling to an English-speaking country could have served as a motivating factor to persist in her studies, despite her high level of anxiety.

I believe the role of a teacher is not only to provide information to students, but to encourage and inspire them to learn. It's important that teachers engage their students in the language learning process and get them to commit to putting forth effort over the long term, and both of these goals can be accomplished by tapping into students' motivation.

Different students have different motivations. Most of the students in my study were driven by the fact that they had to complete their English studies before they could take other classes at the English medium university. Like it or not, they had to pass the English class before they could study what they wanted to study. This requirement can serve as a source of frustration for some because they can't reach their goal without passing this program. Others, however, see it as a motivation to learn as much as they can so they can eventually understand what is being said in their mainstream university classes.

Teachers need to know what is motivating their students. This is where I feel the coaching approach comes in. Teachers can begin by asking their students what they expect to learn in the class. This can open a dialog in which teachers can discover what's really driving their students.

Teachers may have to gently push students to help them discover their own incentive for taking a proactive role in their education.. For example, a student may say she is taking the class only because she has to—not exactly a strong motivator. However, through additional questions, the teacher could help the student realize that it's in her best interests to make the most of her time in class—after all, she's paying for it.

Regardless of what is motivating students, once students have their motivations at the forefront of their minds, they're more apt to act on them. Here are some sample questions language teachers might ask students to help them recognize and become driven by their motivations:

- *What excites you about learning this new language?*
- *How will learning this language benefit you? What do you hope to do with your new skill of speaking this language?*
- *How can your new language help you in your personal and professional life?*
- *What is your timeline for learning this language?*

Imagine the possibilities when the teacher has the answers to questions like these! By coaching students through strategic questions, teachers can help students triumph over anxiety and reach their potential.

This strategy centers around tapping into *why* students are learning the language and focusing on their motivations. For example, if a student's goal in learning a language is to advance their career, the teacher can assign projects or bring in materials in the target language that are closely related to that student's career goals and interests. This makes the language learning experience more relevant to the student's long-term goals; as the student sees they will use the new language in their work, they'll likely be motivated to learn it. Similarly, if a student is learning a language for fun, the teacher could learn about that student's hobbies and bring in materials that relate to those interests, whether art or playing basketball.

Through a coaching approach, teachers can empower their students to design a plan of action that enables them to take control of their learning. Once students have a plan of action, the teacher can serve as a coach in the class by keeping students accountable in making progress toward their goals.

When talking to students about their goals, teachers should be sure to ask students about their timelines for learning the language and help them make sure that their expectations are realistic. Some students may expect to be very fluent after two semesters of study, and if they're not fluent by that point, they may think that they're failing to reach their goal. By asking coaching questions, teachers can help their students align their expectations with reality.

Encouraging Autonomy

A coaching approach is not only useful in helping students discover and act upon their motivations, but is also an excellent way to help students become more independent and take initiative in their learning. By asking the right questions, teachers can prompt students to think of strategies to address the challenges they face. For example, teachers can ask:

- *What did you learn from this project?*
- *What challenges did you face while completing this project?*
- *How did you overcome those challenges?*
- *If you were assigned a project like this again, what would you do differently so that these challenges would be more manageable?*

Although I hadn't yet learned about the coaching process when I taught English at the university, looking back I see that I used some coaching techniques in the classroom, and these techniques benefitted my students. For instance, when I assigned a project that required students to seek information outside of their textbooks (such as giving a presentation on a "trip of a lifetime"), I'd ask my students what challenges they faced. Often, they'd tell me they'd procrastinated, and as they shared, they were better able to recognize the roadblocks they'd faced and plan how they'd address these challenges in the future.

Practical Tips

In addition to taking a coaching approach with students, there are a number of practical ways that teachers can help their students recognize and overcome anxiety. In this section, I'll speak directly to teachers, suggesting steps they can take in their classrooms. This section can also help the general public understand the importance and complexity of FLA.

As a language teacher, you have a great responsibility: You're laying the foundation for everything students will learn in their new language. You're charged with building a deeply rooted base upon which other teachers can build. Without a solid base, everything that other teachers try to accomplish will crumble. The following tips can help you build a sturdy foundation.

Recognize and Seek to Understand Anxiety in Students

It's crucial that language teachers are able to recognize signs of anxiety in their students. If they don't, how can they address anxiety-related issues in the classroom and identify students who might need help? Some of these signs, both behavioral and physical, often cannot be seen by teachers (or anyone except for the students who are suffering from FLA); nonetheless, it's helpful for teachers to know these signs so they're able to recognize if their students are suffering from FLA. Keep an eye out for the following signs of language anxiety in the classroom.[2]

Behavioral symptoms:

- *disruptive behavior*
- *excessive joking or laughing for no reason or desperately trying to make light of a situation when it's unnecessary or inappropriate to do so*
- *rarely speaking or volunteering to participate*
- *avoiding tests, presentations or other classroom activities in which language abilities are evaluated*
- *self-doubts*

---

2.   Oxford, R. L. (2005). Anxiety and the language learner: New insights. In J. Arnold (Ed.), *Affect in Language Learning* (p. 58). Cambridge, UK: Cambridge University Press.

- *perfectionism*
- *cutting class for no reason*

Physical symptoms:

- *fidgeting*
- *excessively playing with hair or clothing as a nervous reaction when in class*
- *stuttering*
- *lack of concentration*
- *buzzing sound in the ears only when in language class*
- *sweaty palms*
- *heart palpitations*
- *unexplained dizziness, headaches, stomachaches, or pains while in the language class, that go away as class finishes or as students exit the classroom*
- *unexplained body pain or tension during class that fades after class*

Once you've recognized the signs of anxiety in your students, try to determine the causes of this anxiety. Those who suffer from FLA often experience anxiety due to a *combination* of factors related to themselves (individual differences) and the language learning environment. Their anxiety could be exacerbated by your teaching style or by specific exercises that are used in the classroom. As discussed in the sections to follow, questionnaires and student feedback can provide you with a wealth of insight into the causes of students' anxiety. The more information you can gather, the better informed you will be about how you can modify your teaching methods to lessen this anxiety.

Utilize Questionnaires

The questionnaire I developed for my study, the AFLAQ, can be a useful tool for language teachers in Saudi Arabia, as well as in the surrounding Gulf States due to similarities in culture and educational systems. In Western contexts, the Foreign Language Classroom Anxiety Scale (FLCAS), introduced in Chapter Four, is helpful. By administering questionnaires like these to students, teachers can gain a better understanding of the situations that cause anxiety in their students, as well as identify students who are experiencing FLA. Armed with this knowledge, teachers can then take a more proactive approach by modifying their teaching methods and reaching out to students struggling with FLA.

If you're teaching in the Gulf States, consider administering the AFLAQ at the beginning of the semester, and then again halfway through it. This can help you determine if students' anxiety is lessening, and if changes you've made in the classroom are helping to reduce it. Please note that it's best to administer the questionnaire anonymously so that students feel free to express what they really think without fear of judgment—or loss of face. (If you are teaching in the West, you could use the same process but administer the FLCAS.)

Obtain Students' Feedback

In addition to using the information you glean from the AFLAQ or FLCAS, ask students what they enjoy in class, as well as what they don't like, so that you can tailor your methods accordingly. The students in my case studies were very in tune with what made them anxious—I didn't anticipate they'd be so insightful—and if their teacher had only talked with them, it might have changed her way of teaching. Your students are likely full of insight as well.

Like many of the students I observed, your students might not volunteer their opinions about what goes on in the classroom. By asking them for feedback, you let them know that you want to know what they think and you give them an opportunity to express concerns in a way that they know is acceptable in the classroom environment.

In addition to asking your students about the elements of class they like or dislike, ask them what they're looking for in a teacher. You may be surprised by what comes out of this discussion. Your students' feedback can help you define your role as a teacher—for example, you may discover how much and what type of input or feedback your students are seeking.

If you're taking a coaching approach, you'll also learn about your students' preferences in the classroom through your conversations. Take these into consideration when planning lessons, and look for ways to incorporate students' suggestions.

Modify Methods

Questionnaires like the AFLAQ and the FLCAS can provide you with incredibly valuable insight into what parts of the learning process cause the most anxiety in your students. Equipped with this information, you can find out what situations, assignments, or challenges are causing that stress. And, as a crucial next step, you can then make changes in the classroom that can help to alleviate some of this anxiety and encourage learning.

For example, if you administer the AFLAQ and learn that students strongly agree that classroom presentations cause them anxiety, you can lessen the weight that presentations are given in determining students' grades. Or, you could start the year by having students give a few presentations for which you give feedback (in writing, not in front of peers) but not grades. This would give your students the opportunity to experience giving presentations, getting positive and constructive feedback, without concern for grades. Using strategies from coaching, you could ask students to identify what it is about giving presentations that makes them nervous, and then develop strategies that correspond to your students' concerns. The idea is to open the lines of communication with your students and receive their input. As a result, you'll increase your students' motivation to learn and work, because they'll feel they have a say and play an active role in their own education. The end result will be more autonomous learners.

It's important to note that modifying your teaching methods to help lessen your students' anxiety does *not* mean setting low expectations for your students, nor does it mean avoiding pushing your students to try new things that may be out of their comfort zones. Rather, you're helping your students overcome their anxiety so that they can meet difficult challenges, try tasks outside their comfort zones, and ultimately succeed as language learners.

Openly Discuss FLA

By opening a conversation about anxiety, teachers can demonstrate that they're aware of how their students are feeling. An open discussion of FLA can also help students recognize that they're struggling with anxiety related to language learning— the first step in overcoming their anxiety. Students who are aware of their FLA can set more realistic expectations regarding their use of language in the classroom, which can help them dodge feelings of failure when they face challenges. Discussing FLA can also help normalize students' experiences, as students realize that they're not alone in their anxiety.

Talk openly with your students about the anxiety and fears they're likely to face, not only at the beginning of the course but also throughout the semester. Validate their feelings and let them know that frequent errors, stuttering, forgetting words, and other signs of anxiety are common and normal. It's also important to demonstrate empathy for your students. Let them know that you understand the challenge they're facing and cut them a little slack accordingly.

Encourage your students to talk about their anxiety openly in class. As students share what they're going through, they realize that they're not alone in their feelings and struggles. They might also come up with creative ideas for reducing and dealing with these feelings.

It can also be helpful to utilize technology in ways that encourage students to talk about their anxiety. For example, set up an online chatroom in which students can share their thoughts or fears anonymously so that they do not risk losing face in front of other classmates. You could even establish a private Facebook page where the class can interact and share the tools and strategies they have found helpful when learning material from class, such as vocabulary or grammar. If you set up this group in a way that encourages the use of the new, target language, you could foster an environment in which students work *collaboratively* to express new ideas in the target language. Or, such a group could just be a fun venue— for example, a place to share funny news stories or cartoons published in the target language so that students are engaging with the language in a low-pressure, entertaining way with no associated grades or evaluations.

Clarify Expectations

Clear expectations can help reduce anxiety. This is true in everything from small, in-class assignments to course grades. That's why it's important to clearly explain each activity so that students know what's expected of them. It's also important to clearly explain the basis for students' grades, and make it clear that students aren't graded on how well they speak during practice sessions in class. Students are more likely to feel self-confident and motivated in the foreign language classroom if they understand the classroom procedures and what is expected of them; this decreases ambiguity and the anxiety that can come with uncertainty.[3]

Remember that students who are learning new languages often fear being evaluated for their speaking and language skills. This can be true not only during formal evaluation, but also during language practice: They may feel that every word they speak is an opportunity for the teacher to grade or judge them. As a result, students can feel intimidated by and fearful of the teacher, and may hesitate to speak because they don't want to be evaluated negatively. To help students get past the fear of speaking, you could create a system in which participation in class in the target language is rewarded (i.e., points toward a grade are earned), but issues like pronunciation and grammar are ignored. In such a system, students receive credit and eventually an improved grade if they're striving to contribute to the class. Of course, students' contributions need to be relevant: if a student mentions the weather during a discussion of historical literature, that student does not earn credit. The idea is to invite and reward students' efforts to communicate in the new language, even if that effort includes mispronounced words, hand gestures, and words from the students' native language.

---

3.   Dörnyei, Z. (2005). *The Psychology of the Language Learner*. London: Lawrence Earlbaum.

Choose Materials Wisely

Choose materials that help students learn. Horwitz recommends using video rather than audio resources for students who are still in the early stages of language learning, because videos allow students to see facial expressions, gestures, and the setting of a conversation, all of which can help them understand what's being said.[4] In addition, use materials that allow students to hear natural patterns of speech, rather than the recorded conversations that accompany most language textbooks. This will allow students to get a feel for the way the language is used in real-life settings and better enable them to understand native speakers in everyday situations.

Explain the Benefits

Introduce new classroom activities so that students understand what each exercise is designed to teach them. When beginning a new classroom activity or project, take the time to explain the benefits associated with the activity, so that students understand what they'll gain from it. This can help them become more aware of their role in their learning and take responsibility for that role.

Explaining the benefits is also helpful when assigning homework—students need to know that you're not giving them work just to keep them busy. In addition, if they know

---

4. Horwitz, E. K. (2008). *Becoming a Language Teacher: A Practical Guide to Second Language Learning and Teaching.* Boston, MA: Pearson Education, Inc.

the purpose of an assignment, they may be better able to focus their attention and energy, enabling them to take some control over their education and become more independent learners. Let students know that their homework will give them an opportunity to practice what they've learned in class that day, and that by completing it, they can help prepare themselves for tests as well as lay the foundation to learn new things.

This concept can apply to any subject. Take math, for example. You could tell students that knowing how to add will come in handy when they're at the supermarket buying their favorite candy, ice cream, or gum. They'll be able to determine how much all of their items will cost before they get to the cashier so they can be sure they'll have enough money to pay for these things. As these students progress in their math skills, they will start learning about percentages. You could say to them, "Don't you hate it when you add up the cost of all the items in your basket and make sure you have enough to pay for everything, only to find out that there is something called tax? Tax is a percentage of the amount you already added up, and if you know how to calculate it, you can know exactly how much you'll need to pay at the cash register. You can also use percentages to figure out the cost of something on sale. So, percentages will be very useful!" Regardless of the subject, make the learning material very relevant to the students so they get on board with their learning journeys.

Offer Positive Feedback and Encouragement

Don't underestimate the impact of encouragement. Over and over, the students in my case studies (especially those in Level 3) shared that they needed the teacher to encourage them and pay attention to their efforts without being excessively critical when they made mistakes.

Encourage students to try to speak, even if they aren't sure of the words, and make it clear that mistakes aren't a sign of failure. Over time, positive feedback and encouragement may help reduce students' anxiety, and, in turn, may help students develop self-confidence.[5] But, without support, students can lose motivation (as was the case with Tamara), become depressed or even start hating their classes (as Farida did).

Always offer your students reassurance, whether they're answering questions or giving a presentation. Even a small expression of encouragement from the teacher can have a big impact. Sara was extremely happy to hear her teacher say "Great," after she and several classmates gave a presentation, and she shared that even seeing her teacher smiling and taking interest was encouraging to her: "I felt satisfied midway through the presentation when I looked at the teacher

---

5. Khaldieh, S. A. (2000). Learning strategies and writing processes of proficient vs. less-proficient learners of Arabic. *Foreign Language Annals*, *33*, 522-534.

and found her smiling and looking like she was genuinely interested."

In addition to giving verbal feedback, be aware of your body language and facial expressions. As Sara stated, her teacher's smile and expression of interest made a big impact on how she felt while giving her in-class presentation. Simply having a teacher who is an attentive, open, and friendly listener can serve as a great motivator and help a student relax. Smiling and nodding signal to a student that they are on the right track, even if the student is stumbling over words or making other errors.

There's no doubt that feedback is needed in the classroom: Students need constructive criticism to improve. The way in which teachers give this feedback makes all the difference, and too much of it can have a negative effect on the students' self-esteem. When students in Middle Eastern classrooms receive constructive criticism in front of the class, they may try to save face or pretend that they grasped a concept even though, in reality, they don't understand a thing because their anxiety has already kicked in. While this isn't true for everyone, it's a good example of how overcorrection can negatively impact the language learner.

Avoid overcorrecting students in class or being unnecessarily critical as students who receive too much negative feedback may become more hesitant to speak in their new language. It's vital that students feel the teacher is treating them kindly. Sara told me about an instance in which a teacher extensively corrected one of her classmates, and shared that if she had been in the other student's position, she would have simply quit instead of dealing with the constant corrections. Other students echoed Sara's feelings. Tamara explained that she felt encouraged if the teacher was polite and corrected mistakes nicely; but, if the teacher incessantly corrects and talks over the students, she feels the teacher is picking on them. She would not want to be picked on in front of her classmates, and agreed that she would rather refuse to speak than be constantly corrected in front of classmates.

It is very important that teachers find ways to correct students that are positive rather than critical. For instance, you could give an example of the wrong way to use a word and play a game with students in which they discover why it's wrong. This approach engages the students in a fun way. As they analyze the example, they'll come up with the answer themselves rather than passively receiving correction from the teacher. So, not only will you be offering constructive feedback, you'll encourage students to participate in class and be autonomous learners—and to have fun doing it!

Respect the Learner

Respect for your students will go a long way in helping to reduce their anxiety. Cultivate an environment in the classroom in which each student feels respected, valued, and heard.

An important part of demonstrating respect for each student is ensuring that each one receives feedback and attention, even those who tend to remain quiet in class. As mentioned earlier, several of the students in my case studies told me that they felt that teachers played favorites, focusing on the more vocal students. Be intentional about investing in every student, encouraging each one to participate and giving each one opportunities to do so.

Students—particularly those who tend to be quiet or reserved—need to know they can participate in class without being interrupted or talked over. While this is important in every classroom—after all, there are always students who are more talkative and those who are quieter—it's especially vital in a foreign language classroom, where students are often already hesitant to speak in class. You must create an environment in which a student who is trying to speak isn't interrupted, either by the other students or by you. Students need time to think before speaking, and some students need more time than others. It is important that they are given that time. For instance, Sara shared with me that she needed more time to think through what she was going to say before speaking in class. If she didn't get enough time to think and other students jumped in, she was never able to participate; that, too, frustrated her. If students aren't given the opportunity to speak, how can they improve?

Another aspect of creating an environment in which students feel respected and valued is remaining positive and not judging your students. Statements like, "You should be able to do this by now—you're not working hard enough," are a big blow to students' motivation even if they are said in a nice way. Keep your responses positive to help keep your students' anxiety at bay.

Don't Ban Students' Native Language

Don't be too strict when it comes to students' use of their native language in the classroom. While students should certainly be encouraged to use the language they're seeking to learn in class, there will be times when they simply don't have the words to communicate their thoughts in this language. By not prohibiting students' native language, you enable students to express themselves even when they're limited by their ability in their new language. As we've already seen, not being able to clearly express thoughts can be a major cause of anxiety for students, and by allowing students to use their native language on occasion, you can help to lessen this cause for anxiety, especially at the beginning levels of language learning.

I returned to London a few days after my talk at the conference organized by the English Department of the Ministry of Education in Saudi Arabia. A week later, I was walking on Edgware Road when I heard someone calling me: "Dr. Taghreed!" As my name is not very common in London, I assumed that this person was calling for me. I turned around and a woman greeted me. "You don't remember me, but I attended your talk," she said. "I was in Saudi Arabia. I was one of the teachers in the audience." My initial shock of hearing my name being shouted on a busy London street soon turned to a smile.

She went on to tell me that my talk was an eye-opener for her. She shared, "I, as a teacher, never thought such a thing [FLA] existed, let alone that students can be negatively affected by it. I now know how important it is to ask "why" and "what" questions and to pay attention to my teaching style."

Teachers, it's my hope that this chapter has been eye-opening, informative, and thought-provoking for you as well.

Chapter Eight 8

How Students Can Help Themselves Overcome FLA

Despite the huge role that teachers play in FLA, students aren't powerless or merely at the mercy of their instructors—far from it! In this chapter, I'll speak directly to students, explaining how they can overcome anxiety and set themselves up for language learning success.

First and foremost, students struggling with FLA need to recognize that they're experiencing anxiety. As mentioned in the last chapter, signs of FLA include the following:

Behavioral symptoms:
- *disruptive behavior*
- *excessive joking or laughing for no reason or desperately trying to make light of a situation when it's unnecessary or inappropriate to do so*
- *rarely speaking or volunteering to participate*
- *avoiding tests, presentations or other classroom activities in which language abilities are evaluated*
- *self-doubts*
- *perfectionism*
- *cutting class for no reason*

Physical symptoms:
- *fidgeting*
- *excessively playing with hair or clothing as a nervous reaction when in class*
- *stuttering*

- *lack of concentration*
- *buzzing sound in the ears only when in language class*
- *sweaty palms*
- *heart palpitations*
- *unexplained dizziness, headaches, stomachaches, or pains while in the language class, that go away as class finishes or as you exit the classroom*
- *unexplained body pain or tension during class that fades after class*

Are you experiencing any of these symptoms? If so, seriously consider whether you might have FLA. While a headache certainly isn't a sure sign that you're dealing with language anxiety, symptoms like these can serve as red flags that alert you to feelings of anxiety, or increase your awareness of them. Especially pay attention to the timing of your symptoms—do they appear when the language class starts but fade away after class? Do you regularly have stomachaches or heart palpitations, but only on the day of your language class? Once you're aware of your FLA (if you have it), you can accept it, come to understand it, and use the following techniques to help reduce its effect on you.

Accept and Seek to Understand Your Anxiety

If you're experiencing anxiety, you may wonder, *Am I the only one feeling this way? Why do I feel anxiety in my language class but not in other classes—is there something wrong with me? Am I just stupid when it comes to learning a new language? Am I just a bad student?* Rest assured, the answer to each of these questions is, "NO!"

Feeling anxiety while learning a foreign language is common, and a lot of people experience it. So if you do suffer from language anxiety, you are not alone. (As you've read, even I suffer from it.) Many other students have anxiety too, even if they don't talk about it. Feeling anxiety is not an indication that there's something wrong with you or that you're a subpar student. While knowing these things may not ease your anxiety, it can help you accept it—and accepting that you have FLA is the first step in overcoming it. Please remember that we typically thrive with a bit of anxiety in our daily lives to help us accomplish tasks and achieve our goals—if we were not anxious at all, we might simply sit around without a care in the world. The key is having the right amount of anxiety: If we don't have enough, we aren't motivated, but if we have too much, it will hinder us from benefitting from the language learning experience. We want a healthy dose of anxiety to motivate us and challenge us to accomplish our language learning goals.

Once you've recognized and accepted that you have FLA, think about which situations make you feel anxious. Do you feel nervous while giving a presentation in front of the class? While answering the teacher's questions? When taking exams in the language class?

Taking the AFLAQ (copies in both Arabic and English are included at the end of this book) or the FLCAS can be a great way to explore what makes you anxious. Reflect on why you answered each question as you did and why certain situations make you more anxious than others. Identifying the causes of your language anxiety can be a big help in overcoming it. As a certified coach, I work with my students and clients to explore their thoughts on certain things because I know that thoughts create feelings, which ultimately create emotions. These emotions are what we are trying to deal with, and awareness of these emotions is the first step toward being in control or proactively moving forward. In the language learning context, this awareness allows you to continue to learn your target language and reach your ultimate goals.

Another simple way to identify your anxiety is to ask yourself open-ended questions. Avoid asking yes-no close-ended questions as these tend to stall your reflections in their tracks.

Try asking, "What worries do I have in the language class?" This type of question opens up an opportunity for you to brainstorm with yourself and reflect on the situations that make you anxious as a language learner. Try to ask "what" and "how" questions as "why" questions are sometimes hard to answer; you may not know why you feel the way you do, but you probably know how a situation makes you feel or what triggers that feeling.

After you've identified what triggers your language anxiety, you can look for ways to reduce it. Throughout this chapter, you'll learn practical strategies that can help you ease and overcome your FLA.

Know that Mistakes are Part of Learning

Mistakes are essential to learning, not only in the language learning process, but in life in general. Whether you're learning to play volleyball or play the piano, you get better when you goof up and gain skill by practicing. The same is true in language learning: By mispronouncing and misusing words you learn to say and use them correctly. Remember, mistakes are what push us to change, and we need change to overcome our anxiety.

Mistakes are good. You can't learn without them. However, knowing this in your head and embracing it in your heart are two very different things. Often, the brain knows that making mistakes is beneficial, but the heart says that errors are something to be feared and avoided at all costs. Although fear of mistakes is common, this fear can get in the way of learning.

Now that I'm living in San Francisco, I constantly hear about the startup companies all around me—I guess San Francisco could be called the birthplace of startups. To satisfy my curiosity about these companies, I took a course called "How to Start a Startup" at Stanford University. What I heard from all the fantastic speakers, including the founders of PayPal, Jawbone, and Airbnb, to name a few, was that you need to be sleeping, eating, and breathing your idea or cause in order for it to succeed! This sort of focus and determination is the result of being 100 percent committed—with both your head and your heart. So, if we were to take the startup company plan of action and bring it into the language classroom, then we need to be focused and determined to learn the language, in both our minds and our hearts.

In coaching, we say the heart and the brain need to be aligned. If you're torn between what your brain wants (to learn a language) and what your heart fears (making mistakes), you won't give 100 percent of your effort to accomplish your goal. You must give that 100 percent to overcome obstacles, not only in language learning but also in life.

So, how can you focus and align your mind and heart? First, you need to notice your emotions so that you can gain better insight about yourself and discover how to cope more effectively. How can you change your feelings of language anxiety if you don't know what your feelings are, when they occur, and what triggers them? Let's take my Turkish language learning experience as an example. As a researcher in the field of FLA, I am aware of language anxiety, what it entails, and all its symptoms. Yet, I still suffered from it when I was taking Turkish classes. However, I was able to pinpoint my FLA triggers and when they occurred; knowing these triggers, I managed to coach myself through my anxiety. (On one occasion, I recognized that I needed some external help and reached out to a coach—you read our conversation earlier.) I cannot say that I am completely over my FLA, but that's not necessarily a bad thing: Remember, we all need a moderate dose of anxiety to do anything in life. But, I've learned to change the habits that brought on my language anxiety.

This should be the aim for all language anxiety sufferers: Get in touch with your thoughts! In my case, my mind had a goal of language learning, but my heart was filled with negative emotions as the process of learning was taking a toll on my work and family. Only when I confronted these emotions and changed them was I able to get back on track and make progress toward the language learning goal in my mind. I changed my schedule to take Turkish lessons at the cultural center once a week on Saturday mornings instead of five days a week at 8 a.m., which required me to rush to class and not spend time with my youngest son in the morning. That's just one example of many, but when that burden was off my shoulders, I was able to give 100 percent in my Saturday morning Turkish class and really enjoy it.

Asking yourself the right questions can help you move past fear so that your mind and your heart are aligned. Try asking yourself:

- *What am I trying to achieve in the language classroom?*
- *What is stopping me from achieving my language learning goal?*
- *What will it be like to achieve my goal of language learning?*
- *How important is it to not make mistakes while learning a language?*
- *What's the worst thing that could happen if I make a mistake in the language class?*
- *What's the best thing that could happen as a result of making mistakes in the language class?*
- *How will I feel once I've overcome my language anxiety?*

Talk About It

Don't keep your feelings of anxiety to yourself. If you share them with others in your class, you'll likely find that others are struggling with many of the same things that you find challenging. While discovering that you're not alone in your feelings can be incredibly helpful in and of itself, talking about your anxiety can also bring another big benefit: As you and your classmates discuss your experiences, you may be able to help each other come up with ways to actually *reduce* the anxiety you feel.

Don't talk about your anxiety with just your fellow students: Talk to your teacher as well, explaining the situations that make you feel anxious. You have insight that can help your teachers, but it's only helpful if you share. By making them aware of the things that cause you anxiety, you give them the opportunity to take your anxiety into account. While you can't guarantee how they will respond, your teachers won't be able to help and support you in overcoming your anxiety if they aren't aware of it.

In addition, speak up about the things that would help you feel less anxious. For example, if it would help you to have more time to formulate your answer when the teacher asks you a question in class, then let the teacher know. Or, let's say that you get nervous when you have to listen to a tape-recorded conversation and then answer questions about that conversation. Speak up and ask your language teacher to give you more time to listen to the tape and to repeat the tape a couple of times so that everyone gets to hear it and understand its content.

I realize that some students don't feel comfortable doing this and that some teachers are easier to talk to than others. However, if just one or two students speak up, it can benefit the entire class. Why not be one of those students?

Set Realistic Expectations

If you set expectations that are too high, you're setting yourself up for disappointment. While it's great to have high aspirations, if you expect yourself to become fluent in a new language after just a semester or two, you'll fail in your own mind no matter how hard you study. (It can be done, but it's exceedingly rare.) When you set unrealistic goals for yourself, you put far more pressure on yourself than you need to; and, as you struggle to meet too-high expectations, your anxiety will only increase.

For the majority of language learners, myself included, it's reasonable to expect it to take about a year (two or three semesters) to pick up a foreign language that isn't the primary language being used in your surroundings, depending on how much personal time and effort you invest in learning that language. Your opportunities to use the new language outside of class are very limited, which makes practicing the language a lot more difficult. Hence, you'll likely need a longer period of time to master the language than you would if you were able to put your new skills to use in real life. When I taught English, some of my Level 2 students wanted to be proficient in the language in one semester so they could continue their education at the English medium university. It simply wasn't realistic—for them or for you. You're not going to pick up on a new language in one semester, especially when you have limited opportunities to use that language.

On the other hand, when you're immersed in the language you're learning and surrounded by its corresponding culture, you can become fluent in a shorter period of time. I must confess that I would have learned Turkish a lot faster if I was actually practicing the language instead of just relying on watching the Turkish soap opera. I tried desperately to find Turkish people around me so I could practice my Turkish with them, but it's very hard when you are working, researching, raising a family, and taking classes, all while trying to learn a new language.

Instead of making it your goal to become proficient, set smaller, measurable goals that will help you learn. Make your goals as specific as you can—you'll be more likely to follow through. Think about it: If you make it your goal to exercise more, you're unlikely to change your behavior. However, if you make it your goal to hit the gym three times a week, you have something specific to shoot for. The same is true for language learning goals. Determine to take specific steps that will help you learn. For example, you could make it your goal to watch the news in the language you're trying to learn three nights a week or commit to practicing in front of a mirror after each class. Remember to break your goal into smaller steps as I demonstrated earlier in this chapter.

Find Your Motivation

I firmly believe that if you put your mind to something, you can do it. But, before you can put your mind to something, you need to find your motivation. What's driving you to learn a language? Remember to ask yourself empowering, open-ended questions such as:

- *Why am I learning the new language?*
- *What's my motive to continue learning the language?*
- *What will I gain from learning the new language?*

These questions can help you discover your motivation, as well as clarify your goals. Perhaps you want a better job that requires being fluent in a new language. Maybe you want to communicate clearly when you travel. Or, perhaps you just want to be able to follow a certain TV show like I did, whether for pleasure or research. No one can tell you whether your motive to learn a language is valid—only you can know this.

In my case, I was intrigued by the sudden interest everyone around me had in Turkey due to the popularity of the Turkish TV drama series, and was driven by a desire to research and embark on a journey of self-exploration as I learned the language. I wanted to experience firsthand what my students reported about anxiety in their language class, and to see if I, too, would be as affected by anxiety as they were. Sure enough, I was, even though I never thought I would be. But, I was able to overcome this anxiety because I had a clear motivation to learn Turkish and I was flexible in my strategies for achieving my goals.

My journey has continued for over a year, and motivation still plays a big role. I have achieved my original goal, am now completely in love with the language, and often visit Turkey for pleasure and to practice the language, as well as give presentations (in English) at language learning conferences about my research. I am not completely fluent in Turkish, but it's now a matter of practicing the language and getting the hang of using it. I continue to learn the language for my own pleasure, and I watch the Turkish TV series as much as I can. (Remember, you have to regularly practice and hear a language so you don't lose it and your ears remain familiar with the sounds and intonations of the language.) As I always say to my boys, the more languages you have, the more people you can communicate with! As an extrovert, I love to talk with people of different nationalities and cultures. As you know, I have already lived in several countries and traveled a great deal, so I won't let a language barrier get in the way of communication. My desire to communicate and my love for languages continue to drive me to learn.

At the end of the day, you're the only one who has the right to judge whether your motivation is reasonable, silly, or perfectly valid. It's all up to you, the language learner. When you understand your motivation, you're more compelled to be personally invested in your education. With motivation, language learning isn't just a "have to," it's a "want to"!

"Want to" comes from within you and indicates that you are in control of what you choose to do, while "have to" implies that you are somehow being forced to do something. That's why it's important to make sure that your motivation is coming from a want, as being motivated by a want puts you in control.

But, what if your reason for learning a language is based on a have to—for example, you need to learn a new language to advance in your career? How can you maintain your motivation? My suggestion is to dig deeper and ask yourself:

- *Since I have to learn this language, what good can come*

out of it? (List as many things as you can.)

- *How can these results of language learning benefit me in my personal life?*

By asking you to answer these questions, I'm trying to get you to buy in to the language learning process. I want you to feel that you're not forced to learn, and that the skills you're learning will benefit your personal life one way or another. Then, it will be a win-win situation. While you're still learning the language because you need to, you're doing it on your own terms. So, you are in control and you get something in return. You have a choice to learn the language or not, and this freedom of choice is absolutely empowering.

Coach Yourself

In the last chapter, I mentioned how a coaching perspective can help teachers assist their students in discovering their motivation. Guess what? You can coach yourself!

By asking yourself the right questions you can clarify your goals in learning a new language, as well as come up with strategies that can help you manage and overcome your anxiety and succeed as a language learner. That's what I've been doing as I continue studying Turkish, and you can do it, too.

Ask yourself:

- *Why am I studying this language?*
- *What are my goals for learning this language?*
- *What's my timeline for learning this language?*
- *What will learning this language help me achieve?*
- *How will I know when I've achieved my goals? Or, what needs to happen in order for me to realize that I have achieved my goals?*
- *What steps will I take to achieve my goals?*
- *How will I be accountable?*

The whole point of having a coach is to have accountability, and you can provide this accountability for yourself when you act as your own coach. So, how can you hold yourself accountable?

Seek an Accountability Partner

A friend or colleague can be your coach (as long as they're willing to hold your feet to the fire). Share your goals—and your timeline for meeting them—with a friend or colleague, and ask them to check in with you to see if you reached your goal by your deadline. For example, each week you might make it your goal to memorize a certain number of vocabulary words and practice using them in a variety of sentences. By the end of the week, you'd report your progress (or lack thereof) to your accountability partner. If you reached your goal for the week, your friend should acknowledge your achievement and offer congratulations. On the other hand, if you fell short, then you must explain to your friend why you did not reach your goal as well as how you plan to remedy the situation so you don't fall behind on your larger, long-term language learning goals.

If you're into social media and like to make your efforts public in order to keep yourself accountable, try an online option. Using websites like StickK (www.stickk.com), you can set up a system for holding yourself accountable for any goal you want to achieve. You select a goal (again, make it specific and measurable), and then determine the stakes. For example, what happens if you don't learn 10 new words per week? You might require yourself to contribute $5 to a charity or savings account for every week you fail to meet your goal. If you use StickK, you get a referee: a person you know and trust who will monitor you. You can also post your goals and successes on Facebook or other social media so that friends and loved ones can cheer you on. If enough people use sites like these to help them achieve their own individual goals— whether in language learning, fitness or anything else—the process can snowball as they encourage each other.

The key is to set achievable, concrete goals and realistic timeframes in which to accomplish them, and then to have someone hold you accountable. Having an accountability partner can be similar to having a personal trainer at the gym.

You're not only paying for the trainer's time and expertise, you're also paying for them to hold you accountable. So, you respect their time and tend to show up to work out when you said you would. You ultimately agree with your personal trainer about what you need to do in order to reach your goal, and the timeline in which you want to accomplish this goal. Your trainer then keeps you on track.

Timelines and Procrastination

Timelines are crucial. I know that if I don't set deadlines for myself, I tend to procrastinate indefinitely. So, even if something does not have a deadline, I tend to make one up for myself to keep me focused—otherwise I would be nicknamed the "Queen of Procrastination!"

Remember that procrastination is considered a sign of anxiety. You may be afraid of starting something or it may be that, deep down, your heart isn't in it. When you put off a task rather than jumping in and getting to work, there's a reason. When you find yourself procrastinating with a language learning task, ask yourself questions such as:

- *What's making me procrastinate?*
- *What am I afraid of in doing this?*
- *What's the worst thing that can happen if I don't achieve*

my goal?

- *What's the best thing that can happen if I do achieve my goal?*

I can't predict the future, but I am sure that you will have answers for these questions. You may not recognize these answers right away, so dig deep for them. Your reason for procrastinating could be something silly or something big. We are all different and we each have our own ways of dealing with the thoughts that trigger our emotions. So, the more you are in tune with yourself and your thoughts, the more easily your mind and your emotions will align.

Develop Self-Confidence by Improving Your Language Skills

One of the most powerful things you can do to decrease your anxiety is to improve your language skills. As you become more skilled and practiced in your new language, your self-confidence will increase, which can dramatically lessen anxiety.

Several times while I was studying Turkish, I inadvertently threw Turkish words into casual conversations with my English- or Arabic-speaking friends. (If you ask me why, I have no clue!) This unintentional act impressed my non-Turkish-speaking friends, and their comments and praise drove my confidence through the roof. I'm sure I gave them the impression that I was fluent in Turkish, which was not quite true yet. Although I usually denied that I was fluent, I must admit that these comments boosted my confidence! As a result, I was more energetic and motivated to learn more Turkish.

Learning a language doesn't take place only in the classroom. To follow are several practical strategies for practicing your skills and gaining confidence in your new language.

Use Social Media to Your Advantage

If you're a social media fanatic, why not find a chat room for language learners? Or, better yet, start a chat room for your language class so that you and your classmates can practice outside of class in a fun, non-academic way. My Turkish class started a closed Facebook page where class members could post interesting facts about the Turkish language, as well as YouTube lessons that they found useful. Strategies like these enable students to use language in an authentic way without worrying about grades or what the teacher will think about mistakes.

By creating a social network with your classmates, you are eliminating the formal barriers that may be inhibiting you in class, and you and your classmates will likely be more at ease with each other. Your main objective when posting will be to simply get your message across, rather than worrying if you're saying everything correctly.

One could argue that students don't learn how to correct their mistakes if there is no supervision, but my answer to this is, "Please do make mistakes!" It is only by making mistakes are we able to learn how to use a language correctly.

You can learn so much from your peers, especially when they're your friends. Research has demonstrated that learning a language from friends is more effective than learning in an academic setting.[1] A major reason for this is that it's fun! And, wanting to belong to a community or interact with certain friends can provide an extra boost of motivation.

Watch Foreign Films and TV Shows

Watch films and TV shows in the language you're trying to learn so your ear becomes more accustomed to that language. But, don't be a passive viewer. Pay attention to words and sentence structures, stopping the movie or program if you can to try to figure out what's being said. Little by little, you'll get used to the intonation and use of the language, even if you don't

---

1. Clément, R., Major, L., Gardner, R. C., & Smythe, P. C. (1977). Attitudes and motivation in second language acquisition: An investigation of Ontario francophones. Working Papers on Bilingualism, 12, 1-20.

understand all of the words. And, as you begin to grasp what's being said, you'll gain additional motivation to comprehend that language so that you can follow what's going on.

That's just what happened to me when I watched the Turkish TV series. I started watching it to get used to hearing the language, with Arabic subtitles to keep me interested in the plot. Since I was drawn in to the plot, I looked forward to the next episode. With each episode I was absorbing the words, intonations, and usage of the language. All this kept me coming back to learn more and more.

Why watch TV in your target language rather than just listening to the radio or podcasts? When you're only listening, you need to rely heavily on the scope of your vocabulary. Watching television is easier because there are visual clues regarding what is being said, though you still may not understand everything. When I went to Turkish class, I simply memorized words. But, when I heard these same words on the Turkish TV show, it was very different. Before I watched the show, the words were just sequences of letters on paper, but in the context of the show, they were used appropriately in conversation (not how I would have used them!) and given life and meaning. When you watch television, vocabulary and grammar start to make sense. Yes, you must learn your vocabulary, but I suspect that, as was the case for me, it will begin to fall into place when you watch TV in your target language.

Set a goal for yourself for each program you watch in your target language. For example, you could determine to pick up on five to 10 words and practice saying them. So, have a paper and pencil handy while watching the program. Try to watch programs that are recorded so you have the luxury of rewinding. You can hear each word a couple of times, pick up on visual clues about the word's meaning, and see how the words are used.

One challenge presented by this strategy is not knowing how to spell a word in the new language. While learning Turkish I would phonetically spell out the Turkish words I heard in Arabic or English, and then ask my language teacher how to spell them. Sometimes she'd laugh and ask where I was getting these words and how I knew their meanings without being able to look them up. Needless to say, I learned a lot from that Turkish drama series.

Practice in Front of a Mirror

Talk to yourself! Stand in front of a mirror and have a conversation with yourself in the foreign language, verbalizing out loud rather than just having a conversation with yourself in your head. I guarantee that trying to communicate an idea out loud is very different than doing the same thing silently in your mind. You may remember that earlier in this book, I mentioned having a short conversation with myself in the car on my way to Turkish class so I could impress my teacher with my fluency in using the language. Well, gaining fluency is the point of this exercise: It gets you used to talking and hearing your own voice in the language you're seeking to learn.

You may also recall that I did not do so well in class after practicing in my car that day. I think this is because I was concerned about what the people around me were thinking about me. I was not focused at all. That's why I'm suggesting that you practice in front of the mirror or in a room all by yourself. This way, you won't be concerned about what others are thinking about you. You won't be inhibited when you're the only one listening. And you'll be better able to recognize mistakes when you can actually hear yourself speaking.

Improve Your Presentation Skills

If you find that giving a presentation in the language class is difficult for you and triggers your anxiety, try to practice giving the presentation a couple of times in front of a friend or family member with whom you're comfortable. If you don't want to practice in front of friends or family members, then there is always the good old reliable mirror!

Many of the techniques that can help you prepare for a

presentation in your language class are the same strategies that can be used to address a fear of public speaking. Let's look at some practical pointers to make presentations in your language class a bit easier.

Before the presentation:

- *Keep in mind that your anxiety may get worse before it gets better. Keep working on it, and do not give up. Change is hard work!*
- *Give yourself a big vote of confidence that you can overcome your language anxiety. This will boost your self-confidence, which is essential to your success as a language learner.*
- *Break your fear of giving a presentation into small parts, and face them one step at a time. For example, if you're most worried about pronunciation, repeatedly practice your vocabulary out loud until you master the pronunciation. This will ease one part of your fear of giving the language presentation. Then continue with the next aspect of your anxiety you've identified, working on each part one step at a time.*
- *Whatever you do, avoid blame. Do not blame yourself for any reason whatsoever. Be patient and keep practicing— it will get better with practice! Remember that by now, you know more than the average person on the street because you're learning more than one language.*

On the day of the presentation:

- *Sit alone and try to imagine your presentation going well. Sometimes visualization helps people become familiar with a situation so that when that situation actually comes about in real life it feels old hat. If you picture yourself giving a presentation ahead of time, by the time you get to the real thing you may feel as if you've already done it, and that the presentation you're giving in front of the class is just a repeat of the original one—a big weight is lifted from your shoulders.*

- *Try a five-minute centering technique. This may include going into a quiet room, being silent, and just focusing on breathing deeply to clarify your mind. An exercise like this can help you calm down and focus on the presentation. Deep breathing can be especially helpful in limiting stuttering. I've witnessed this firsthand with students.*

- *If looking at your classmates during the presentation makes you very anxious, try to focus on a point in the center of the room so you don't lose your train of thought.*

After the presentation:

- *Accept your performance as is, and do not expect perfection. Remember that mistakes are what push us to change, and we need to change to overcome our anxiety.*

- *Reward yourself! Acknowledge that you've done your very*

best and that you deserve a reward, whether small or big. All of these tips will help keep your self-esteem and self-confidence high. Both are essential for overcoming anxiety in general, and especially language anxiety.

Be an Actor

Charlemagne said, "To have another language is to possess a second soul." I agree completely. As discussed in Chapter Six, learning a new language involves gaining a second identity that's rooted in the culture of that language. Practice assuming your second identity by going out with a friend and talking in your new language, and try to immerse yourself in that language by spending time in a community that uses it.

In short, this requires some sort of acting on your behalf. Yes, *acting!* I say that because being truly fluent in a new language means being able to function while using it, and this may require that you behave in ways that are different than you're used to. You must learn not only what to say, but also what is acceptable to do or say. Sometimes the differences between the culture of your native language and the culture of the language you're learning are minimal, and you won't have to act that much. But, when there are massive differences, you have to be a good actor in order to function within your new language.

In my case, the Turkish culture was not very different from the Arabic culture, so I did not have to be a good actor while learning Turkish. However, the Arabic language and culture and the English language and culture could not be more different. I act and speak in English very differently than I would speak and act in Arabic. (I must say, I am a very good actress since I got started at such a young age!) When I'm operating in English, I tend to be more easygoing and not worry about making mistakes. If I do make a mistake, I just joke about it and carry on. But when I'm speaking in Arabic, I have to consider whether the situation is formal or informal, and am careful not to make mistakes so that I don't lose the respect of my peers. This gets me in trouble because, since I travel and live internationally, the barriers between cultures can get diluted—it's hard to keep track of the script sometimes!

Whether you have to act a little or a lot, find ways to immerse yourself in the language you're trying to learn. As you do, you'll gain a second soul.

Make it Fun

If you're studying a language in a very formal setting, it's not likely you'll be able to alter the environment of the classroom. But, you do have control over the way you practice outside of class. Make it fun by watching TV and movies in the foreign language or setting up a regular practice time with a friend. Hang out with friends who already speak your new language and do your best to communicate with them without relying on your native language. You could also go to a restaurant where your new language is spoken and try ordering and talking with the waiter in that language.

If you can, immerse yourself in your new language. Visit a country where the language is spoken or spend a day in a community in your own country where that language is predominant.

In the previous chapter, I mentioned that Hind's motivation played a role in her successfully passing the English course. I think something else also contributed to her success. Unlike many students, Hind didn't see her teacher as the sole cause of her anxiety. Instead, she recognized that students play a role in student-teacher dynamics and she took partial responsibility for her experiences in class.

By recognizing the role you play in your anxiety and finding your motivation, you, too, can set yourself up for success. Although there are many things you can't change about the foreign language learning environment, you can change how you approach it. And, when you do, you can overcome your anxiety.

Chapter Nine 9

Conclusion

Don't let anxiety prevent you from learning a language.

Yes, anxiety can be a barrier, but it can be overcome—I'm proof! The keys to managing and moving past FLA lie in incorporating accountability, changing your thoughts that bring up negative feelings, and adding pleasure to the language learning process.

If you're studying a language, make an action plan that will help you reach your goal. Remember, you can break down your goal into to smaller steps to make it achievable. For example, aim to learn a certain number of words per week. I did this in my Turkish studies. Each week I committed to learning 10 new words and their usage. To make sure I stayed on track, I'd email a friend to say whether I'd achieved my weekly goal. I also had a back-up plan in case I didn't accomplish my goal for a given week: I'd make up the words I'd missed the next week. Knowing that I'd have to learn more words the following week if I didn't learn them in the current week motivated me to hit my target from the start and not fall behind.

By setting a goal with a date, you hold yourself accountable for your own progress. Goals and accountability look different for each person. Deep down, everyone knows what they can and can't do, and we need to be honest with ourselves in setting goals and holding ourselves accountable. It's vital that you find your own accountability and motivation. If I tried to impose a set of goals on you, you'd likely get annoyed with them or not stick to the plan at all. Remember to base your motivation in a want rather than a need. If you are learning due to a need, try to see how learning a language will benefit you in the long run so you can make learning a "want to" rather than a "have to."

It's also crucial that you link language learning with pleasure—language learning extends beyond the classroom. Make it a point to meet some people whose native language is the one you're trying to learn and converse with them. Enjoy the process. We naturally want to blend in, and this innate desire can help motivate you to learn to communicate in the language your friends are speaking, as well as pick up on it in a way that's natural and fun.

It's my hope that more language programs will begin adopting methods that allow students to learn in a way that's natural and based on learning to communicate. Katharine B. Nielson, chief education officer at a language learning company based in New York City, suggests that language students should be taught how to communicate in the target language as opposed to being taught rules of grammar. Early research on this method indicates this approach is highly effective. The approach was used successfully in 2006 to teach Spanish to United States Customs and Border Patrol officers. In addition, Europeans have seen success when using foreign languages to teach non-language subjects.[1]

Remember, you're far from powerless in overcoming anxiety! Never give in to fear or self-doubt. If you do, you'll miss out on the delight of talking to and coming to understand people from different cultures, whether in your own country or on an adventure abroad.

Ups and downs are part of the language learning process. The key is to persevere through the downs and to be proactive in moving forward. When you do, you can achieve a dream, even one that goes against all odds—just like I did.

---

1.   Nielson, K. B. (2014). The best way to learn a foreign language is the opposite of the usual way. *Forbes*. Retrieved from http://www.forbes.com/sites/forbesleadershipforum/2014/04/22/the-best-way-to-learn-a-foreign-language-is-the-opposite-of-the-usual-way/

Acknowledgments

I would like to thank the English medium university that so graciously allowed me to observe English language classes, talk with teachers, and spend time with students. I am especially indebted to the brave English language students who openly shared their thoughts, concerns, and fears with me. They gave me great insight into how foreign language anxiety affects them, and their experiences fueled my curiosity, driving me to keep exploring and to ultimately examine my own experiences in learning a foreign language. Without their willingness to disclose their experiences (without fear of losing face!), which motivated me to dig deeper into the personal experience of FLA, this book would not have been possible.

Hopefully, our combined efforts will help reduce FLA for other students.

Appendix

Arabic Foreign Language Anxiety Questionnaire (AFLAQ)

Please indicate how strongly you agree or disagree with each statement.

Response Scale	Strongly Agree	Agree	Neither Agree/ Disagree	Dis- agree	Strongly Disagree
Score	[5]	[4]	[3]	[2]	[1]
1 I feel nervous when I can't write or express myself in the foreign language.					
2 I feel anxious when the teacher asks me a question that I have not prepared for.					
3 I feel nervous and confused when the language teacher is unsuccessful in explaining the lesson.					
4 I fear speaking or asking the teacher in my foreign language class.					
5 I feel anxious when listening to a passage in my listening/speaking class.					
6 I get nervous when there is a lot of vocabulary that I don't understand being used in my foreign language class.					
7 I feel nervous using the foreign language outside of the college or class.					
8 I am not nervous speaking the foreign language in front of my classmates.					
9 I get nervous when I arrive late to class or the day following my absence.					
10 I get anxious when there are too many foreign language students registered in my class.					

Response Scale	Strongly Agree	Agree	Neither Agree/ Disagree	Dis- agree	Strongly Disagree
Score	[5]	[4]	[3]	[2]	[1]
11 I feel anxious when I see classmates better than me in my foreign language class.					
12 I feel comfortable in speaking with my foreign language teacher.					
13 I feel anxious in reading/writing and grammar class					
14 I get upset due to the method of testing in the foreign language class					
15 I get anxious when I feel that I can't speak well in front of other language students not in my class					
16 I get nervous when looking at my grades.					
17 I get nervous and confused when I am speaking in my language class.					
18 During language class, I find myself thinking about things that have nothing to do with the course.					
19 I tremble when I know that I'm going to be called on in language class.					
20 I feel nervous when talking in the foreign language to someone I just met.					
21 I get nervous when the language teacher gives us a lot of things to do in so little time.					
22 I feel overwhelmed by the number of grammatical rules I have to learn in the foreign language.					
23 I fear pronouncing words incorrectly in my foreign language class.					

193

Response Scale	Strongly Agree	Agree	Neither Agree/ Disagree	Dis-agree	Strongly Disagree
Score	[5]	[4]	[3]	[2]	[1]
24 I fear failing my foreign language class.					
25 I feel low self-confidence about speaking the foreign language in front of the class.					
26 I feel anxious about speaking the foreign language in front of other students.					
27 I feel nervous when I am around more experienced foreign language users.					
28 I don't feel anxious when learning a foreign language.					
29 In language class, I can get so nervous I forget things I know.					
30 I feel anxious when I don't understand what the teacher is saying in the foreign language.					
31 I feel anxious when I want to volunteer to say something but can't find the proper words to say it in my foreign language class.					
32 I feel nervous at exam time.					
33 I feel nervous when standing or giving a presentation in front of the class.					

Note: For a more detailed description of the development and use of this questionnaire, please see Al-Saraj, T. M. (2014). Revisiting the Foreign Language Classroom Anxiety Scale (FLCAS): The anxiety of female English language learners in Saudi Arabia. *L2 Journal, 6*(1), 50-76.

استبيان

فضلاً اختر افضل اجابة للعبارات التالية:

لا أوافق بشدة	لا أوافق	لا أوافق ولا اختلف	أوافق	أوافق بشدة	العبارات	
					أشعر بالتوتر عندما لا أستطيع أن أكتب أو أعبّر عن نفسي باللّغة الإنجليزية.	1
					أشعر بالقلق عندما يسألني المدرّس أي سؤال لم أكن مستعدًا له.	2
					أشعر بالتوتر و التشوش الفكري عندما يفشل مدرّس اللّغة الإنجليزية في شرح الدّرس.	3
					أخاف التكلّم أو سؤال المدرّس في حصص اللغة الإنجليزية.	4
					أشعر بالقلق عندما أستمع إلى قطعة في حصة الاستماع / التحدث باللغة الإنجليزية.	5
					أصبح متوترًا عندما يكون هناك الكثير من المفردات التي لا أفهمها مستخدمة في فصول اللغة الإنجليزية.	6
					أشعر بالتوتر عند استخدام اللّغة الإنجليزية خارج الكلّيّة أو الفصل.	7
					أنا غير متوتر عندما أتحدّث باللّغة الإنجليزية أمام زملائي.	8
					أصبح متوترًا عندما أصل متأخّرًا للصف أو في اليوم التالي بعد غيابي.	9
					أصبح قلقًا عندما يكون هناك كثير من طلبة اللغة الإنجليزية مسجّلين في صفي.	10
					أشعر بالقلق عندما أرى زملائي أفضل مني في فصول اللغة الإنجليزية.	11
					أشعر بالارتياح بالتحدث مع مدرّس اللغة الإنجليزية.	12
					أشعر بالقلق في حصة القراءة / الكتابة و القواعد باللغة الإنجليزية.	13
					أصبح منزعجًا بسبب طريقة الاختبار في اللغة الإنجليزية.	14
					أصبح قلقًا عندما أشعر أنني لا أتحدث جيّدًا باللغة الإنجليزية أمام طلبة اللّغة الآخرين الذين ليسوا في صفي.	15
					أصبح متوترًا عندما أنظر إلى درجاتي.	16
					أصبح متوترًا و مشوش الفكر عندما أتحدّث في حصص اللغة الإنجليزية.	17
					أثناء فصول اللّغة الإنجليزية، أجد نفسي في بعض الأحيان أفكر في أشياء لا تمتّ للمنهج بصلة.	18
					أرتعش عندما أعرف أنني ساستدعى للإجابة على سؤال في حصص اللّغة الإنجليزية.	19

Recommended Reading

Al-Saraj, T. M. (2014). Revisiting the Foreign Language Classroom Anxiety Scale (FLCAS): The anxiety of female English language learners in Saudi Arabia. L2 Journal, 6(1), 50-76.

Gregersen, T. & MacIntyre, P.D. (2014). Capitalizing on Language Learners' Individuality: From Premise to Practice. Bristol, UK: Multilingual Matters.

Horwitz, E. K. (1986). Preliminary evidence for the reliability and validity of a foreign language anxiety scale. TESOL Quarterly, 20(3), 559-562.